THE MIND OF A PYONEER

JOURNEY OF THE CULTIVATION PHASE 1

BRYAN SCOTT BURRELL II

authorHOUSE

AuthorHouse™
1663 Liberty Drive
Bloomington, IN 47403
www.authorhouse.com
Phone: 833-262-8899

Published by AuthorHouse 05/17/2021

ISBN: 978-1-6655-1810-9 (sc)
ISBN: 978-1-6655-1809-3 (e)

BURRELL ENTERPRISE BUSINESS INFORMATION
Website: PyoneerApparel.com/PyoneerApparel.net
Fitness Accountability App: "Pyoneer Push-Up Challenge"
LinkedIN: Bryan Burrell
Email: Armond25Burrell @gmail.com

Facebook Pages:	Instagram Pages:	Twitter Accounts:
Bryan AB Burrell	@Ceo_Burrell	@Ceo_Burrell
Pyoneer_Clothing LLC	@Burrell_Enterprise	@BurrellEnterpr1
Lady_Pyoneer LLC	@Pyoneer_Clothing	@Pyoneer1
Sports Intrigued LLC	@Lady_Pyoneer	@LadyPyoneer
The Real Nyte Train	@Sports_Intrigued	@IntriguedSports
	@TheRealNyteTrain	@NyteTrain88

FaceBook Groups:	TikTok Accounts:	Snap Chat Accounts:
Pyoneer Clothing Fan Page	@PyoneerNation	@Ceo_Burrell
Sports Intrigued	@Ceo_Burrell	@Pyoneer2020
	@Burrell_Enterprise	@Lady Pyoneer
	@SportsIntrigued	@PyoneerNation
	@NyteTrain88	@NyteTrain88

Tumblr Accounts:	Myspace Accounts:	LLC's
@Ceo_Burrell	Burrell Enterprise	Burrell Enterprise LLC
@PyoneerNation	Pyoneer	Pyoneer LLC
	Lady Pyoneer	Lady Pyoneer LLC
		Sports Intrigued LLC
		Nyte Train LLC
		Pyoneer Publishing LLC
		Pyoneer Printing LLC
		Pyoneer Promotions LLC

Email Addresses:
Armond25Burell@gmailcom
PyoneerApparel@gmail.com
SportsIntrigued@Gmail.com
TheRealNyteTrain@gmail.com
BryanBuysHomes@gmail.com
ValuedPropertyBuying@Gmail.com

ACKNOWLEDGMENTS

I would like to acknowledge everyone in my life that I know personally, and all those that I may have come in acquaintance with. I would rather not mention any names, because I would not want to leave anyone out. All of you, in one way or another, have made an impact on my life, and I am blessed to have known and met such great people throughout my years in life. I acknowledge that I am not perfect, and that I do not know everything. I understand that I may have made mistakes in life and may have also wronged people in some cases being ignorant and not understanding the impact we have on one another; whether that is good or bad. I now understand how valuable we are to one another. I understand that we should always strive to help build one another up in a positive way, and that we as people, we live, we learn, and we continue pressing towards our destiny. I hope that as you press toward your destiny in life, that maybe this book can help you in ways even I could not imagine. Thank you again, to all those in my life, and to all you who even dare to finish reading this book. Peace to you all and may you all be blessed.

DEDICATION

I would like to dedicate this book to my family, my friends, and everyone that decides to read this book. To my beautiful daughters and their beautiful mother, who stood by my side through this entire process. To my close friends and those who believed in me and supported me from the start. To the city of Toledo, Ohio, and everyone in my community that has given me great support thus far. I hope we all make it through this book together, learning and taking anything we can from it that will benefit our own personal lives. I hope this read will inspire more authors, more entrepreneurs, and more business minded people. People that will apply whatever they can, from the things that they might have learned in this book to their everyday lives. I dedicate this book to all my elders, the ones who have come before me, the ones who have paved the way in all aspects of life for me. The ones who gave my generation any sound wisdom that we possess today. Lastly, and certainly not least, I dedicate this book to the youth. The youth who essentially are our future! The future generation of this world. Future leaders, future rulers, future entrepreneurs, and future businessmen & women. The future Pyoneer's of this world; I dedicate this book to you all.

INTRODUCTION

When I first outlined this book, I thought it was going to be a biography. The way this book came about, was me trying to start my own business, a business I would begin by flipping cars and being active in the real estate market. The plan was to use my knowledge buying cars and properties that would later yield a financial return in profit. Starting this business of mine, ideas began to flow and the entrepreneur within started to take over. I came up with my own company that would host a trail of subsidiary companies beneath it. I designed logos for a lot of these companies I had in mind. I wrote a business plan on how to accomplish it all. I developed a fitness app that came to mind during the process of constructing this business plan. During this time, I was curious as to how and why I was thinking the way I was thinking at the time. Why was I so business minded, and how was I this business inclined? Why was I so business, business, business all of a sudden? Where was all this knowledge, planning, desire, and all of these strategies coming from?

That is when I wrote down all the previous jobs I worked for in the past that came to mind. Going further, I thought of anything in my past that may have been essential to the shaping of this newfound business knowledge I was now operating in. I began to write each job down and all the experiences and knowledge I acquired or encountered thus far, that has cultivated my thinking into the businessman and entrepreneur I am today. It was right then that I noticed I had a book on my hands. Although I was not quite sure what kind of book it would be, or how I would compose it; I was sure that there was more than enough knowledge I had from firsthand experience alone that could be beneficial to any like-minded person. Assessing everything I wrote down my goal was to extract what I knew, putting it all out in book form.

I will take the time to say that this is not your typical novel. My plan was not to write nor compose this book the way any normal person does or would. No, this is not that particular kind of literature. This book is more of a journal. A journal for myself and other like mind minded people that do not mind perhaps a bit of learning along with a great read. I illustrated this book the exact way it came off my mind; that is why it is called "The Mind of a Pyoneer." I do not think my thinking is average, and with that said I chose to personally compose and illustrate this book exactly the way I saw fit. Therefore, please bear with me as I try to take what is in my mind to try give it to you in book form.

I wanted to take what I knew about business, marketing, and entrepreneurship, and explain how over the course of time I have learned to excel in each. I wanted to offer the knowledge I have, (from a first-hand cultivated experience process,) in hopes of someone being able to benefit from something they have learned in this book. I remember my first book purchase and everything I learned from it. My first book purchase cost me $19.99, and probably was the biggest and best investment I could have ever made at the time. Becoming an author, myself, and understanding that everything comes full circle, there really is no telling where my life would have been had I not bought that book that day.

During the time of writing this book I was asked numerous times what the book was about. After being asked so many times, the question itself kind of helped me narrow down as to what this book is about, and what I wanted to convey to the audience. Concluding I determined that this book is a "Business & Marketing 101, Becoming an Entrepreneur," memoir. Created to help, motivate and inspire like-minded business people, entrepreneurs, and hopefully to inspire more people to start reading more than they already are. I hope also to possibly inspire more people to become authors themselves, or to even start a business of their own one day. As we journey through this book, I hope you all can learn something that will benefit you in your everyday lives. I hope we all make it to the end of this book together, taking whatever it is necessary, that will benefit us moving forward in our personal lives… Without further ado, "let the journey begin."

CHAPTER 1

A PRODUCT OF THE ENVIRONMENT

"A Diamond in the Making"

As a kid I lived with my mother. I remember moving around a lot from one home to another. Born and raised in Toledo, Ohio in a household of five, (my mother, my brother, two sisters and myself.) By third grade I would say is when we finally found a place we would call home for years to come. We moved over to the eastside of Toledo into an apartment complex in a small urban village. A community that would shape and develop me into everything I would later become.

It took time for my brother and I to meet any friends in this new area we had now lived in. Being new to the community was a challenge itself. With that said, I remember my brother and I would get into fights with all the other boys our age, simply because we were technically still "outsiders". Being new kids in the community immediately gave us the outcast title. We had not yet become what I would call "family," in this new village we were now in. After settling in for a few months, and after a handful of fist fights with the other boys that lived in the village, we would all soon develop a bond and a brotherhood that would last forever. I would assume that us growing up with one another and living so close together is what forced us all to deal with one another.

It would not be until we first started playing football with each other, that we would realize our true chemistry, and potential to make one another better. The game of football is what brought out a lot of this chemistry and potential for us to be great as a unit, rather than individually. That

1

same game of football taught us so many valuable lifelong lessons that some of us may still use today. It taught us how to connect and rely on one another. It taught us how to do our own individual job on the football field for a greater collective team goal. We learned how to trust and fight for one another, and how to give something your everything in order to accomplish a set goal. We learned how to sacrifice and put our own desires aside, in order to achieve greatness as a unit.

We won together. We lost together. We had to hold one another up if ever they were down in spirit for any reason. We also pushed and inspired one another, and as the saying goes "iron sharpens iron," we sharpened one another. It didn't take long for this chemistry to kick in either. I remember it like it was yesterday! The day I got introduced to the game of football. My 3rd grade year is when I remember moving and settling into this new community; this new village we had now lived in. At the time, I didn't really know much about football, and none the less I was not interested.

By fourth grade I was getting a bit bigger in size, but I was still too small to try out. Not sure why, but my mom had taken my brother and I out to a football practice one day at the school we were now attending, (Garfield Elementary.) It was my first "hands-on" and "in-person," football experience. Watching these guys run around the football field attacking one another in physical combat was all new to me. Being new to this sport and never seeing such a thing, I have to say, it intrigued me a bit. It gave me the desire to somehow want to even be a part of it. I wanted to learn what these guys were doing. My brother and I still had not really made any friends so maybe this was me looking to be a part of something outside of my immediate family. Unfortunately, the coach told my mom that we were still too small to play that year, and that maybe she should try bringing us back the following season.

Coming back to try out my fifth-grade year I was full of excitement. I had just learned about the sport roughly a year before and it was now time to hopefully and finally play on a team. I had grown in size from my fourth-grade year to my fifth-grade year, so I was sure size would not turn me away this year. Our first day at tryouts, my excitement was immediately stripped away from me. I was blindsided by the news I received that day. I was told that any player who had been "assigned" to the next grade as opposed to being "promoted," were all academically ineligible to play that year. I was then sent home in grief only in hopes of being able to play the game of football my 6th grade year. It would be a year for me as a kid to make sure I did everything correct and necessary to finally step foot on to a football field as a player. To finally become a member of a football team. This was it, and there was no other option.

Leaving no doubts, I was promoted from the fifth grade to the sixth grade and could now finally try out for our football team. A bit nervous of it being my first time, the game was not too hard to catch on to. As long as hitting and tackling others was a part of the game and legal in this sport, I was fine. To go even further, I actually became a natural at it. Tackling people came easy once we got into equipment. With a helmet and a set of shoulder pads, I was ready for battle. All I needed to know was to hit the man with the ball, and that was it, end of the discussion. Hitting players and tackling players became my forte. So much so that one of my defensive coaches wanted to give me a nickname. I remember he asked me what my nickname was, and I replied "Armond." Armond was the name my mother had given me at birth right before my father changed it to his name; "Bryan."

Impressed by my tackling ability, my coach said that I needed a new nickname. He then asked me what nickname I want to be called, and with a short pause of thought, I answered, "just call me A.B." He went on to ask why it was that I chose A.B, and I replied: "it stands for Armond Burrell." At the time, my mom and everyone else I knew called me Armond, so I became accustomed to hearing and liking it. Growing up, none of my friends ever called me Bryan, so when the coach gave me the option to nickname myself, A.B was the best acronym I could come up with, and it stuck with me ever since.

I became "A.B." a football sensation! One hitting and tackling machine. I knew my role, and I knew what I was good at. I knew what I did best, and I knew what I brought to our team as an individual that essentially made us greater as a unit; that essentially put us in a place to be successful. I knew and understood my responsibility. I knew what my 1/11 for the team was, (1/11 being 1 player's responsibility on the football field, out of 11 players total on the field of play, on one's team.) We all did! We all knew our role and understood the importance of each. We knew each role and we knew that each player had their own responsibility, and we knew the importance of each role for us all to accomplish our collective goal, (a championship trophy.) We knew that no player and no role meant more than our team goal. Each role, and each player were just as important as the next role and the next player; and we embraced that!

Our first year playing together we made it to be one of the last 4 teams standing. We were in the playoffs competing for the championship trophy, and were one game away. Being that it was our first year playing together, we had chemistry indeed, and we knew one other well enough but we had not yet discovered our true potential. Still, we made it to the playoffs, and one game away; one play away from the championship game, it would all end up being a defining night for us all for years to come. We were on defense, and all there was left for us to do was to stop our opponent from scoring a single touchdown. The other team was only about several yards away from scoring their touchdown. It was one play, one game, and only several yards away from the end zone, with all the money on the line. It was time for me to now help my team reach the championship game my first year playing the game of football. Hoping to start the year of a new era, a new dynasty of some sort, this was my time to help bring all this about, and I was ready for it. It was our time to make it happen. It was our time to be great.

Before the ball was snapped, a teammate of mine had a feeling that the ball was going to come my way. I was playing the right outside linebacker position, and my teammate who had the gut feeling was playing the left outside linebacker. He asked if we could switch sides for just this one play, and as much as I wanted to switch him, my thought was that if the play does in fact come my way, that I would indeed make the stop or make the tackle. What I did not account for was my speed. I knew tackling was not an issue for me, unfortunately for me on this play, I happened to be on the side that had the most field, with more space to run on, and to be frank, I wasn't the fastest guy around, and I certainly was not the fastest guy on our team. My teammate who made the suggestion to switch sides was a lot faster than I and should have been on the side I was on for sure, but I chose to remain on the side I was aligned on in hopes of taking matters in my own hands.

Without a doubt, the ball came to my side. It was a toss to the outside, and although I knew that I did not have ridiculously fast speed, I did not adjust myself wide enough, (prior to the ball being snapped,) to compensate for the lack of speed I had; and what do you know, TOUCHDOWN! They scored the ball on my side. I cost my team a chance at a championship game my first year playing on a football team. Devastating enough, and hurt at our core as young men playing this game, it would not be long before we shook that funk off and got back to the drawing board. You see, we knew what we did, and we knew what we had; and deep down we knew what we should have accomplished. We had chemistry, and we trusted one another. We worked hard and we built a foundation on preparation and dedication. We went through ups and downs together that year. Most of all, we developed a confidence like no other heading into that next season.

A confidence that inspired us to predict what our record would be that very next season! It was at our banquet that same season that we ended up losing in the playoffs when this prediction occurred. While at our banquet we vowed not to lose a single game the following season. Directly in front of our parents, our coach told everyone at the banquet that day, that we refuse to lose next season. This statement came the very same day we lost that playoff game. Straightway after losing that game, we had our normal post game team huddle to talk about how our season went and also about our future plans for the next season. We were all so furious and let down, but our coach also saw something in us that year, as did we. He knew what he had, and he also knew that he would almost have the exact same group of players all coming back the following season. I'm sure he knew, and we all knew, that things would be a different story the next time around. It was then when he told us that we will refuse to lose next year, and foolish enough, we believe him. We all knew exactly what he knew. We knew exactly what we had and who we had coming back the following season. We also knew exactly what we should have accomplished that year, therefore his words were more truthful to us than just us hoping or assuming we would go undefeated.

After our banquet and telling our parents that we refuse to lose next season, we went a step further. As a team we went out and got shirts made that even stated this very thing! Our shirts read something like this: "Refuse to Lose Wildcats," followed by the year of the upcoming season on it. A statement that would set the tone of the very way we played the game of football at the time. A statement we would have to live up to. We were just that confident in what we had and what we were going to do, and you couldn't tell us anything.

Declaring to go 8-0 undefeated was a long shot, especially coming from a group of kids; but that is exactly what we ended up doing! We went 8-0 undefeated, and to make things even better, no team scored on us all season up until the championship game, when our opponents only scored once and we outscored them, scoring multiple times putting the game out of reach by a fair distance. All in all, we won and we did what we set out to do. We had a set goal, we put the work in, we even declared what we were going to do as kids, and we went and got the job done. Who would have thought, a group of kids from an urban village, that didn't even like one another when they met would all finally win their first football championship trophy together; and we did it all in style, might I add.

This would be the last time I would ever play football with this group of young men; this group of players, this group of brothers. Football was all I knew, and these guys were the guys I learned to play it with. These were the guys I grew up with playing football with every day; getting better with each day, sharpening one another and challenging one another to evolve. Challenging one another to be great. I thought we would all grow up to play professional football one day. In my head we were all good enough to do so, but I guess not all things work out the way we would like them to. By eighth grade my family and I had now moved across town to a different area. I did not play football in the 8th grade, but I did play my 9th grade year as a freshman in high school. Originally, I was raised on the eastside of Toledo, but now by the time I was in high school we were living on a different side of town. My brother and I would now be playing the game of football with a group of players who we had yet to meet

Being that we were new to the area, we did not know many people at this school. Once again, we had to start over as the new guys. The new face in the area, but it did not take long before my football "hitting and tackling skills," stood out. I played fullback and defensive nose tackle my freshman year in high school. I became one of the key defensive players on the team and that's how I went from being the new guy and being an outcast, to being known and becoming friends with the rest if the team as I done before in elementary football. I was not school popular, just known really by my teammates. My team knew my value, what I did, and what I brought to the team. So that's how again I went from the new guy/outcast, to being friends and known by the rest of the team as I did before in elementary football.

With nothing too special happening for us in football my freshman year I transferred back to a high school over on the east side, (the side of town I grew up on.) My brother and I wanted to get back to the east side so that we could finish playing football on the side of town we grew up on. We figured since we were from that area and had either played with or against these same guys in elementary, that it was only right for us to go back to play with them in high school. By the time we transferred schools we found out that I was ineligible to play football my sophomore year. This was now the second time this had happened to me. I couldn't believe it. Another devastating blow from the game of football for me. I clearly was not learning my lesson, and I would have to do better sooner or later, or else it would ultimately be me paying the price for it in the end.

I couldn't harp on it too much; I could only take responsibility and accountability for what I did or did not do in order to be eligible to play football at the time. Missing a year of football meant that I could now only have a shot at playing varsity for the remaining two years of my high school football career. Two years was more than enough time for me to stand out and make a name for myself in high school football in hopes of getting a football scholarship. Therefore, it was up to me if I was going to make this happen or not. The choice was mine, and to make a long story short, I missed grades my 11th grade year also. It was the worst feeling. You would think by now I would have learned my lesson. I was always a goof ball growing up. Always playing around, not taking much seriously at the time. I was a class clown who always did just enough to get by, and now it was all coming back to bite me.

Not being able to play football 10th and now my 11th grade year also, I began to question myself. I began to question my future and my future plans thereof. All I wanted to do was play football. It was all I knew. I thought I was going to play division 1 football, and then head off to the pros with no problem. With two seasons now down the drain, leaving me with only one season to play, one year to get it right; it was a make-or-break situation for me. By this point I knew my grades would not allow me to play for any division 1 football team. In terms of getting into college

I would be taking what I could at this point. Maybe a division 3 college would allow my grades, but if not, then a junior college would ultimately be my final option if I wanted to continue playing football.

Doing everything necessary and finishing my 11th grade year with the correct grades, I was now able and eligible to play football my 12th grade year in high school. We did not end up having the best year and although it was my first time playing running back, I played the position pretty well that year. Determined for my brother and I, my mom made sure she did everything she could to get us in college. She helped us search for schools that would accept us academically, along with schools that had football programs to offer also. The closest school we came across was a junior college in Buffalo, New York, that my mom and my high school football coach had recently reached out to, in our regard. In a journey of the unknown, this would begin a new chapter in our lives. We were soon to embrace a step into adulthood a long way away from home.

For us, it was like going into a foreign community. An area we knew nothing about and would have to immediately adapt and adjust to; something my brother and I had become used to by now. Like any time before, I would still procrastinate and wait until the last minute to do what needed to be done. My brother and I were recommended by the coach of the college we were going to be attending, to handle all living and housing arrangements months in advance before arrival. We had all summer to do so, but we applied no energy whatsoever at getting this accomplished. All players were to show up weeks before school started to take assessment tests and to get ready for summer camp also. Again, we were to have all our living affairs in order by this time, but my brother and I did not.

Disregarding our lack of effort to handle what we needed to handle as student athletes, my mom, who on a leap of faith felt it necessary for us to still drive up to Buffalo, New York, hoping to get lucky somehow. She had hopes of us finding somewhere to live, I guess. For her son's getting into college, maybe this was a make-or-break moment for her. Packing our things, we set out on a drive to a state we had never been before. No housing arrangements in place, and no clue as to how this would all work out. My mom just wanted my brother and I in college, and my brother and I just wanted to play football. Arriving at our new school we took our assessment test, went to our correct football meetings, and met the other in-coming freshman players also. By then it was time for us to head out in search of somewhere my brother and I could live throughout our time in Buffalo. My mom only had a few days off work before she had to be back, so if something was going to happen, it was going to have to happen fast.

We drove around for hours and still came up short. We could not find anything, and the day was starting to dawn on us. We considered a hotel for a few days, but that would take away from the money we had put aside; money we needed for a place to live. We were budgeting and could not afford to waste any money. Finally, a teammate of ours overheard our situation, and asked his parents if we could stay with them until we found a place to stay for ourselves. Fortunate for us, they were nice enough to say yes, and were open to having us stay with them for a few days. After a few days, my brother and I finally linked up with another teammate who had been looking for a roommate himself. He already had an apartment in the works and could use a couple roommates to split the cost of the rent and utilities bills. Our parents got in contact with one another, and we agreed to split up all the bills between both parties. We got settled into our new apartment, we were miles away from home, and it was now time for a new journey to begin.

CHAPTER 2

THE JOURNEY BEGINS

"A Long Way from Home"

As a freshman in college, I was only seventeen years old. Due to my birthday being in late September, meant that I could start school a year early. There was only one other freshman on our football team that year who was also seventeen years old in college due to his birthday also coming late in the year. He was one of the first friends I met in college aside from my roommate and a couple other teammates. Being seventeen years old in college and in a different state many miles away from home gave me the opportunity to grow outside of the things I was accustomed to back at home.

Growing up, I never got to see a lot of big cities. I never got to do extraordinary things. I only knew Toledo and what Toledo had to offer. I never traveled the country, and I never even flew on a plane as a kid. This was not a bad thing for me, it was just that I had no desire for any of this. I had no need to travel anywhere. Home was enough. I knew my family, my friends, school and football, and all I wanted to do was play professional football. I knew that there was life beyond Toledo, I was not ignorant of the fact; I just never experienced any of it personally, therefore the desire to travel places "for me," just didn't much exist. Moving to Buffalo, New York was the first time I really got to experience life outside of Toledo as an adult. I had just graduated high school, and I was seventeen years old waiting to turn eighteen the following year, (which would have been my sophomore year in college.) I was ready to learn life. I was ready to experience college, then hopefully be heading off to the big league to play professional football.

Honestly speaking, I never really had any back up plan if football didn't go as I hoped. I always heard people say that you need a "plan B," but to me if it's planned, then it has a good chance of happening. Therefore, I kept "plan B," out of the picture until I had to face it directly if all else failed. Otherwise, I was going to play professional football and I was sure of it. I mean after all, I was good enough, and it was all I knew; what could possibly go wrong?

Going into college, I was young but eager to figure this life thing out. I had no idea what my choice of study was going to be. I was there for football, and in my mind an education and a degree would fall second to football once I signed a multi-million-dollar football contract. Therefore, I really didn't give college academics much thought as I was leaving high school heading into my freshman year of college. Being a freshman in college trying to correctly set up my schedule and choosing which major and a minor choice of study to take up was hard itself. Trying to do all of this along with knowing what classes applied for each course itself, was all putting my mind in a frenzy. I could not grasp any of it. Here I was just a seventeen-year-old kid from Toledo, Ohio, who did not really grow up with tremendous educational knowledge trying to figure this all out. Although I was a bright and a smart young man, at heart all I really knew was football because that is all I wanted to do.

Growing up I was under the assumption that in order to make a good living in life you must go to school, graduate high school, go to college, get a college degree, and then use that degree to apply for one of the good money-making jobs that are available. The only other alternatives were making it big in the music business, the acting business, or going professional in sports. Something would have to set you apart, or else you could get lucky hitting the lottery. These were really the only options I saw as a way to make a decent living. I was not very knowledgeable about skills and trades, stocks & bonds, real estate, gold, minerals, agriculture, politics, branding, marketing, advertising, promoting, supply and demand, technology, energy and things like these. I only knew football, and wanted to play it professionally.

College was supposed to teach me things I could only learn in college that I would need in the real world; or at least that's what I thought I was going to college for. To access this hidden knowledge that only professors at one of these colleges could teach me; and to pay an absurd amount of money for this teaching also. College was new to me, and choosing a major course of study meant that I needed to choose a particular course of study that would fall in the area of the career I wanted to be in once finished with college. I was not sure of what study I was supposed to be taking. Asking around, I asked the other players what they chose, in order to see if I could get a better understanding as to what I would choose. My student advisor said that most athletes come in with this same problem. With the sport they plan on playing in mind rather than their academics. She also stated that if I was not sure as to which course I should take, that I could just choose general studies. By taking general studies, I would be taking all the basic requisite classes needed for a college student.

I chose general studies to buy time in learning this whole college ordeal. I was young trying to learn and process it all as it came. I had never really been this far away from home. Everything was a process, but I was stepping into my own man hood, learning things on my own and doing my best to understand life and my purpose of being. I met some great people along the way, and saw some nice things in the process. At seventeen years old, and seeing Niagara Falls for the first time, my mind could now process how vast and open the world could be. This too was new to me. Just seeing the big rush of water spill down so heavily and aggressive was mind blowing. It gave me the feeling that Toledo was not everything my life had to offer. It made me see that I could go beyond what I knew, and in a way, it gave me hope.

Football started to pick up and I started to meet more friends. Not just on the team alone, but at the school also. Our school was literally directly in front of the Buffalo Bill's stadium. We even practiced on their game field once, and on their indoor field a few times, and for a seventeen-year-old kid who had dreamed of playing professional football his entire life, this was finally it! The feeling of practicing where so many legends have practiced and played before was unexplainable. If I never got to play a single down in professional football, then at least I saw and got to practice on a professional field before. Whether or not there were millions of people watching us practice, the feeling was unbelievable.

My freshman year in college I signed up for a lot of classes my 1st and 2nd semester. From all the classes I took that year, what stuck with me most above everything I learned in any of those classes was a conversation I had with a guy while sitting at lunch minding my own business one day. It was a day I didn't think would ever come back around for me. A day I didn't even think to record in my mind, but my mind knew to record it all because almost 15 years later, that conversation is part of the reason I am currently writing this exact book you are reading now!

What I am trying to do is give you a bit of a history lesson about myself, all while explaining specific things that I have learned over the course of time that has shaped and cultivated me into the business minded person I am today. Things that I didn't realize that would come around full circle to benefit me in life and business in today's market. I am trying my best to extract exactly what you, as the reader, can use for your own personal benefit without giving you any unnecessary information. If you have not learned anything from this book so far, I would advise you to take heed to what I am about to share with you concerning the conversation I had at lunch that day.

Out of all the classes I took my freshman year, not very many things stuck with me. When considering the things I was supposed to learn in these college courses my freshman year, it's sad to say but there's just not much I remember from the classes I took that year. If you were to ask me what classes I took that year, I probably could not even tell you which classes they were. There is one thing I do remember from my freshman year that did in fact stick with me. It was that conversation I held with a guy, which took place in our school cafeteria that year. A conversation I will forever remember. I was just getting out of class minding my own business. A bit hungry, I remember heading to our cafeteria by myself.

A man approached me, and we began holding a conversation. He had been in some sort of independent business owner system I was unaware of prior to him explaining it. He began to give me his pitch, and at seventeen years of age fresh out of high school, I had never been pitched before. Everything he said made sense that day, and I was eager to know more. Even though I was all ears and ready to join and sign up, what I did not know at that time, was that everything he said that day would all come full circle for me and in my life in general.

13

The topics he touched on in this conversation were all incorporated within his pitch to get people to become independent business owners themselves, such as himself. He was building his own team of independent business owners, but these same topics would come back full circle for me almost 15 years later around the time I would be starting my own business.

Within this conversation he mentioned words I never heard before at the time. Words like "passive income," and "residual income." These were foreign words for me at the present time, but still I wanted to know more. He went on to explain that people who work 9-5 jobs are essentially trading hours for dollars, which all fall under the category of "passive income." Furthermore, he stated that passive income involves clocking in and clocking out, and ultimately getting paid for the hours you have worked (only.) That there is an invisible ceiling that comes with working a 9-5 job. A ceiling that prevents you from getting paid beyond the number of hours you have submitted for a certain pay period. Meaning you could not get paid unless you were on the clock, and that once you clock out and are off the clock, that is when your pay stops also.

Now on the other hand, you have "residual income." Residual income in my own words, is basically taking a certain period of time, however long the duration calls for, (could be days, could be months, etc.,) but once the work is done and put out to the public, the person or group of people who've accomplished the work will now get paid residually. Lifelong payments that one receives over and over, never having to do the work again because it is now done and released to the public. From that one piece of work, you could now receive residual income for the rest of your life.

For example, think of someone who makes a movie, a song or someone who owns a piece of real estate property. Or even take me for example, (writing this book.) Here I was, getting pitched to become a part of his team, but the universe was teaching me business even when I did not know it. If you would have asked me way back in 2006 during this conversation if I ever thought I would be operating in any form of residual income, or composing a book becoming an author myself, I probably would have laughed at you and walked away. At the time, the only way I saw myself making any real money was if I ended up playing professional football.

There were more things in this conversation that stuck with me also in terms of business-related knowledge. He explained and touched on the "success rate" of most businesses, and why they fail so quickly. I believe he said something in the lines that "95% of all businesses fail within the first 5 years due to lack of knowledge." Now I'm not sure what you got from that, but what I got from it was: "95%, first 5 years, and lack of knowledge." If someone were to again interrupt this conversation I had this day, telling me that I would be running my own business, doing my own research to build & excel my own business, in order to not fall under that "95% business fail rate due to a lack of knowledge," I would not have believed you. Especially if you told me that my company would have nothing to do with this new business, he was introducing me to.

To finish things off, there were still a couple things he mentioned that caught my ear. A few more words and topics that would reside in my memory and would also come full circle regarding me building my own company today. Still pitching me, he explained to me the amount of money, (which was in the millions,) that big companies spend on 30 second commercial advertising alone. He went on to say that "word of mouth" advertising is faster and cheaper, and he explained why.

Again, I'm not sure what rings a bell or sticks with you when I say these things, but what stuck with me was, "millions of dollars, advertising, and word of mouth." All words that would come full circle years later regarding the business I would be starting today. Without making myself seem less intelligent than I am, but at seventeen years old I only thought I knew what the word "advertising" meant. I did not know the impact it has on so many different markets and even in life itself. It would be later when I learned more about advertising and the impact thereof. Doing my own research these days and building my own company I also learned that advertising has everything to do with graphics and design.

I learned how graphics and design has everything to do with "design theory," and how this all has everything to do with economics, socialism, capitalism, and almost everything that pertains to our everyday lives; including politics! Somehow, in one way or another it is all connected, and the better we know this and have an understanding in a lot of these areas, the better we can run, manage, and grow a business to its full potential.

People go to college for many reasons. All I really knew or wanted at the time was football, and that was my reason for going. I had a football background with an entrepreneurial spirit always wishing I could help everyone. Characteristics and traits that would lead me through a series of cultivation phases. A cultivation process that has ultimately shaped me into the well-rounded businessman I am today.

That brief conversation which was probably no more than an hour of talking, has stuck with me to this very day amongst anything else I learned or was even supposed to learn my freshman year in college. I am most thankful for the insight on residual income, passive income, and why 95% of businesses fail within the first 5 years. Knowledge about commercial advertising would all be essential and useful for me years later regarding my own business. With all this said, I did not need to hear any more. He had told me everything I needed to hear that day and I was ready to sign up. I was not thinking of starting my own business nor was I thinking about writing a book yet.

Moving on, I signed up to join his team of independent business owners in hopes of making millions within 2 years of hard work and building my own team of IBO's. After all, I was seventeen, I was young and eager to make money. Away from home trying to figure life out, and then "BOOM," right out of nowhere, I am having a conversation with a guy getting pitched about starting my own business. Hearing words I never heard before, learning about passive income and residual income and seeing how fast I could make money in this business. For me it was a no brainer; he had me at hello.

Before joining his team as an independent owner, the only business cultivation experience I had was when I worked at the golf club prior to going to college. Caddying at the golf course was the first experience I had that gave me the desire to want more in life. It was where I had seen so many wealthy folks, that it intrigued me enough to wonder how I had to be at work 5 to 6 days out the week, but here it was that they could be out golfing almost every day. That thought alone made me curious as to how money really works, as opposed to how I thought it worked. Caddying made me want to know more about what these people did for a living and how they achieved so much success in life.

Joining his team after being invited to a few seminars, I got introduced to so many different people and traveled to more places I'd never been before. He took me everywhere concerning the business. Maybe he saw something in me, or maybe he felt as if I was his protégé or something.

Whatever it was, he would always keep me around. He made sure I attended each seminar and made sure I met the higher ups directly in person.

Attending all the seminars, I was forced to be around like- minded business people. We all wanted to learn ways to grow our independent business. We all wanted to grow and learn what we could from one another in hopes of reaching a certain level that would yield a decent financial return. We were all businessmen and women and entrepreneurs at heart. Being around the business gave us the privilege to associate and be in arm's reach of all the top guns in the company. We could ask questions, gain knowledge, and observe how one another spoke, even down to the way they dressed. I myself personally did so. I observed what they knew and understood about growing their independent business and how I could apply any of it to my independent business at the time.

I even observed their body language and the way they conducted themselves around groups of people who crowded around them for information pertaining the business. For instance, I watched how a certain guy would stand and click his heels together, when giving small circle speeches once the conference was over. Quite the odd thing to do if you ask me, but I needed to know things; I wanted to know what triggered people to do what they did. I was a student of life itself, and I was eager to become successful.

Nevertheless, I sat back learning everything I could because I did not grow up around any of this. I was not raised in business nor was I raised on money.

With no disrespect to anyone working a job, me being around so many motivated and inspiring people, and seeing checks for $25,000 and $75,000 dollars A MONTH, will really make someone re-consider working passively paycheck to paycheck to earn a living. Especially knowing that deep down inside you were created to do more for humanity. Well for me, at this time I always knew that I was an entrepreneur at heart, I just did not yet know which market I would be utilizing my entrepreneur skills in. For that matter alone, I didn't even know what the word market meant at the time. Just a seventeen-year-old kid from an urban area learning from my mistakes as best as I could.

So, one could imagine as to why, after seeing a few of these $25,000 and $75,000-dollar monthly checks (in person,) I decided to call my mom my freshman year in college to explain to her that I had just found a new business system that will make me a millionaire in just 2 years. That I was no longer going to pursue football because I would be building my independent business full time now. That is what I told my mom at seventeen years old, away from home, all the way in Buffalo, New York. The woman who sacrificed and did everything she could, to put us in the position of being able to play college football while pursuing a college degree in the first place. I'm sure that was like a slap in the face after all the hard work and effort she put in for us to be in such a position.

After a long phone conversation of my mom giving me a piece of her mind, I found it in my best interest to let the business go and to finish what we started with football while pursuing my degree. Being an independent business owner at the time was not a priority. I had to finish school, and I had to focus on football hoping that all the effort my mom put in for us would all pay off sooner or later. Though our freshman year would end with a little twist, things still seemed to work out in our favor.

Originally, my brother and I had been accepted to play football at a junior college in Buffalo, New York. As our freshman year was almost up, my brother decided to go to some football combine that would have a lot of college scouts present. He ended up having a good showcase and he impressed the scouts that were in attendance. My brother was then offered scholarship money to attend one of the schools. It was not a full ride scholarship, but at the time we were paying out of pocket to be attending the junior college in Buffalo, New York. My mom got that same group of scouts to offer me some sort of package deal scholarship, and my brother and I packed up as soon as the school year was over and once again, we set out to a new school.

Leaving back memories, coaches, teammates, and friends, we set off to start yet another journey once again. We were transferring schools not knowing where this road would lead us, but we were not afraid of finding out. A road that lead us to Urbana, Ohio. To the university that offered us a scholarship for football. A new environment we would have to adapt and adjust to. A town me and my brother would now be living in playing college football while still pursuing our college degree. Urbana was not quite the town my brother and I was used to though.

It was a lot smaller than the city of Toledo. A bit different and a change of pace for us. It was not the big division 1 college we hoped to attend. The college campus itself felt as if you could go from one side of the campus to the entire other side of the campus in just a matter of minutes. Compared to bigger colleges, this new school of ours was not the school we had hoped for, but I am sure it was not the worst school one could attend. The fact of the matter was, it was still an education nonetheless, and we were going to have to make the best of our time spent there.

CHAPTER 3

THE TRANSFER

"An Entrepreneur at Heart"

By this time, I had a better understanding of a major and a minor in college studies. Asking players and other students, and taking what I learned from my freshman year, I went into my sophomore year with a good grasp on academic studies. Although I still was not quite sure what exact study I would major in, I knew that at heart I was a businessman and an entrepreneur, I just hadn't yet discovered it. You see the thing with me was that I really did not like working for people. For me, it was not a joy to wake up to go build another person's company or dream. Of course, I liked making money, but that was just a means to survive.

I liked helping people, and for the life of me I could not process how someone could be sleeping on a bench or under a bridge with no place of their own. As a kid it honestly did not make sense to me. Why was no one helping these people, or giving them a place to stay? These were thoughts I had as a kid! I wanted to help them all. I wanted to help everyone. That is where going professional came in. I knew that if I went to the pro's, that I could help my family and friends and a lot of these folks that I saw living outon the streets. I remember as a kid I always would say that I would start a home for people who didn't have a place to stay.

Although I do understand that I can't help everyone, and I don't plan on saving the world; it just amazes me looking back, that even as a kid I really had the heart to help a lot of people. That creative and innovative spirit was in me the entire time. I didn't even know that an enterprise had everything to do with innovation, and that being an entrepreneur involved pursuing the things you actually enjoyed. Creating something from within that people do not yet know they need right now, but once the person is finished building it, people will benefit from it.

I learned all this while conducting my own research at the very beginning of starting my own company. I had so many ideas coming all at once and I had to write a business plan for the business I had now come up with. The ideas I had were not just for one company in specific. It was multiple companies, based on a lot of things that have shaped and cultivated my mind into the business mind it is today. The things I am writing about in this very book! It was the knowledge I now had from all the research I had done over the last few years prior to. It was the experience, the knacks and niches, the methods and strategies, and business techniques I learned over time. The knowledge I now have in business, marketing, branding, advertising, and promoting.

It was taking everything I knew and everything I experienced firsthand, putting it all into one business. Which for me ended up being an enterprise that would host a trail of subsidiary companies within the enterprise itself. As a kid, I just wanted to help people and play professional football. I did not know I would be creating something others could benefit from. Although I was fascinated with literature growing up, I never thought I would be composing a book myself. Although I liked fashion but could not afford it much, I never saw myself starting a clothing line; and I definitely never saw myself creating a fitness app, let alone any app for that matter.

All in all, my desire to help people alone was entrepreneurism. It was my fuel, my drive, the motivational factor to believe I was created to do more. Created to bring forth and produce; being more than just a sight to see on a football field. Football would one day be over, and what I brought to life meant more; although football and helping people was not a bad start. Seeing where I am today, writing this book, I look back and it amazes me how much of an entrepreneur at heart I was but not knowing it yet. I guess in my case, timing was everything.

Going with my gut, my sophomore year I chose business as my major. I don't really recall taking a minor study that year. I took a few theater classes because I was big on movies and acting growing up, but truly enough I felt I was a businessman at heart. I mean I knew football, but if that didn't go as I hoped, maybe I could become some big-time actor of some sort. In my head at the time, there were not many options a kid like myself had to choose from. Not quite sure how things would turn out, I knew business was the correct study for me because I did not like working for people. I thought that if I learned business, that one day I could possibly start my own business, working for my own company.

Sophomore year in college was a good year. I was coming off of my first year in college and it was a year of me still finding myself. My brother and I were still playing ball together, but we were still a few hours away from home. At eighteen years old now and a sophomore in college, I was still searching for my purpose of coming to college. I was looking for something or someone to point me in the field I would be in if professional football didn't work out. I wanted to know what my career would be in if all else failed. It was around this time that a backup plan was a wise thing to consider. After all, I was paying to go to school for an education, and not accomplishing that and being in debt would not have made sense to me.

I was in search of finding out where I fit in the working society. There's a saying that "a person who loves what they do does not call it a job simply because they love doing it." I've also heard the saying that "if you follow your heart, the money will follow." I took many courses my sophomore year, but again like freshman year there were certain things above all that chose to stick with me. Things that all came back to my remembrance once I finally started planning and building my own business. I always thought and questioned as to, what and when exactly would I need to use this knowledge I was learning in these college courses.

Not knowing what I was signing up for but knowing I wanted to study business, there waited for me another defining moment that would shape my thinking for the years to come. While taking a business 101 class I remember being taught the power of knowing how to use "power point" software for business projects, lectures and so forth. Above all, I learned how to write a business plan for the very first time. Learning to write a business plan gave me the thought and understanding that if you do the correct research for a business, and also plan and execute correctly, that the business would have a better chance of success.

That if you gain all proper business-related knowledge such as: location, economics, local education, local construction, competitors, current events, knowing your client, targeted audience, return on investments, projections, budgeting, and profit margins; that having a grasp and understanding in these areas, along with thoroughly planning your business and properly executing it (in my opinion,) could very well be a flawless business plan. Outside of learning to write a business plan and how to construct a power point, there was one more thing that stuck with me my sophomore year in college. It did not quite come from any of my classes, but nonetheless it stuck with me to this very day and has a lot to do with me writing this book also. It was a book I purchased from an infomercial I saw late one night; a real estate book teaching people how to become a millionaire in the real estate business. To me, as I watched this infomercial, everything the guy was saying made complete sense, therefore I was compelled to get the book.

I remember staying up late one night watching television in my dorm room when this infomercial came on. A guy who seemed very intelligent regarding real estate came on the television screen that night and began talking about how he made all this money in real estate and how he could even help us, (the viewers,) make millions in real estate also. He was selling a book he wrote for only $19.99! A book that would teach readers exactly how to do what he was doing. Now I may not be the smartest investor, but at eighteen years old, this was the best twenty-dollar back up plan I could purchase, had not football gone the way I hoped. I figured that if I could become a millionaire from spending $19.99 on a book then there was nothing left to consider!

Therefore, I purchased the book, and to give you an understanding of what I felt at the time, I felt like my mind was not fully ready to digest what was in the book. It's like that baby going from milk to meat type of thing. I read the introduction, (which was in fact really good,) and I read a bit of the first couple chapters at the time, but I had to stop reading it after that. I said to myself that I would put it away until I was ready to study it with a more matured mind to have a better understanding of what I was taking in. It would be several years later by the time I decided to actually begin reading and further studying it. I kept it and held on to it and still have it today!

Buying that real estate book my sophomore year in college led me to a series of teachings that have also helped shape and cultivate my business entrepreneur mindset. Had I not purchased that book, I'm not sure where

I would be at in business today. My life would probably be going a different route right now, whether that is for the worst or for the better. All in all, that book purchase was another defining moment for me, and has made a vast impact on my personal life and business life also.

That book purchase along with learning to write a business plan were the essential things that stuck with me as I finished my sophomore year in college. Again, I did not know these things would come full circle in my life today, but they did. The journey would continue though, and there were still more things the universe had in store to reveal to me. The following year my brother did not return to school with me. Up until then, I was never really away from my brother unless it was necessary. We played on the same basketball teams. We played on the same football teams. Being that I started school early, we were even in the same grade and only a year apart from one another.

It was one thing to be seventeen years old leaving my mom in search of figuring life out; but now I was being separated from my brother and having to finish this journey on my own. It was a devastating time for me. I grew up on football. The guy's I grew up playing the sport with were no longer playing the game with me, and now my brother who since growing up, was the only person to still be playing with me; he also, was now parting ways with me. I'd now be finishing school and playing the game of football by myself.

Coming back to school for my third year and this time without my brother, honestly was not very enticing to me. It was more so my coaches and teammates that in a way helped sway my decision to return to school. I met some good friends and people in college that I am still friends with and in contact with today. Even a couple teammates that went on to play professional football themselves. Friends or no friends, my brother was not returning with me so for me, it wasn't the same.

My junior year I would only return for one semester. By the second semester that year, I transferred back home to a university in Toledo. It was the second semester that year when I would learn the last few key things college had to offer me before I dropped out and stopped going, that also helped shape my thinking. Initially I transferred back home because I always wanted to play division 1 college football. My brother was no longer playing alongside me, and I figured why not give it a shot. So, I found a division 1 school back home to transfer to and I was going to walk on to try out for their football team.

Immediately after arriving at the new college university I was now attending, I took the initiative to go see my academic advisor for a bit of guidance. To say the least, my thought was that maybe since this was a bigger school, that the staff in charge could or would have a better handle on academic studies. My advisor was quite the intelligent one. She had me take some sort of placement test that would ultimately reveal which field of study I should be in. The test was very literal and very detail specific with a long list of multiple-choice questions. These questions were basically assessing everything about me to give me an idea of what course of study I fell under.

Completing the assessment test, I was ready to get my results back. I was ready to learn what course of study the assessment results were going to advise me to take. After answering all those questions accordingly, the assessment test revealed that I should major in "Business Entrepreneurship," with a minor in "Business Marketing." She also mentioned that I should take a few electives that would complement my major and minor in the regards of getting a job or starting a career after college.

At the time, I only knew at heart that I was an entrepreneur. Mainly because I wanted to help people, and I knew that I didn't want to work for anyone else. The words market and marketing, were also more words that were foreign to me. Sad to say, but I did not even know or understand what those words meant. Indeed, I heard the words a few times from others, but they weren't words I used in my everyday vocabulary. My advisor did her best to explain to me what they meant, but I was still a bit ignorant of the full understanding. As for direction, my advisor gave me exactly that.

Unfortunately, that second semester of my junior year would end up being my last semester of school. I remember taking an accounting class that semester, and similar to the "marketing" term, accounting also, was another word that was new to me at the time. In this accounting class we learned and were taught about credit, debit, assets and liabilities. Words I was not much familiar with, but words that would also come full circle with my business years later. To say the least, I did not finish that second semester, I stopped going to class midway through the semester and from then I was not sure where life would be taking me.

CHAPTER 4

FOR THE LOVE OF THE GAME

"Back to Football"

Since a young boy first being introduced to the game of football I fell in love. Football was the core of my being, or at least I thought it was. Since then, my only dream was to make it to play professional football. I wanted to be rich and I wanted to be the best at what I did like all the professional football players I saw on television. All in all, I just wanted to help people, and where I come from money was not the easiest thing to obtain. Being able to help my community is what drove me in college and all throughout my life for that matter.

Dropping out of college was not the best ingredient for me to accomplish my dreams, but it would not stop me from becoming the businessman and entrepreneur I was destined to be. Not knowing that everything in the universe was working together for my good, I was still pursuing my football career and no matter how many doors shut on me another door would open. Each door leading me to more learning, more observing, and more experiences that would cultivate me in one way or another. College did not go the way I hoped and expected, but I was still determined and I had not given up on football yet.

My mom had done everything in her power to get me and my brother in college. With all the sacrifices she made and everything she went through to get us in college, was more than enough reason for me to finish pursuing my football career. Although school did not work out the way I hoped it would, none the less I still had breath in my body and I was still alive. I was still hungry for success and I knew I was capable of more than what I was accomplishing at the time. I did not come from wealth, but I had spent a lot of time in the presence of people who were well-off to know that settling for anything less than what I knew I was capable of, was totally unacceptable for me.

Determined to finish what I started I joined a flag football team that a friend of mine invited me to play for. The athletic ability was still inside me, and the desire to make it to play professional football had not fully escaped. By this time, it was a bit tough working a job and playing flag football. I was barely getting by and barely making a living. Finding a job was easy, but finding a job that could pay me my worth, that was the hard part.

I mean after all, being a caddie at a private country club in Toledo, there were times I made $200-$400 bucks a day! Making anything less than this did not sit right with me. We made so much money caddying, but we didn't have a clue on what to do with any of it; we had no investing knowledge whatsoever. Spending it was all we knew. Playing flag football that year I did not think I would enjoy it as much as I did. Things went pretty good for our team that year. So good that even though we were a first-year team, we went on to win our league championship. My body felt great, and I never felt so good as an athlete. I felt as if I was more athletic now for some reason. Even better than I felt in college. This feeling gave me the confidence that there was still hope, and if I felt this good athletically, then there was no point for me to waste it. There was no point of me just sitting around with this hidden talent.

Regret was something I did not want to bear later in life. Being that I was passionate about the game and all I knew was football, I had to find one last opportunity to finish pursuing my football career. In high school, I only played football my freshman and senior year. Due to being academically ineligible, I sat out from football my sophomore and junior year in high school. Being a running back was my desired position growing up, but I was not the fastest so I could only play the full back position on offense. Defense was my specialty, but the running back position is what I desired most.

Though I did earn the job as the starting running back my senior year in high school, we did not have our best season, but it certainly was not the worst year we could have possibly had. We went 5-5 that year, and I played pretty well. It was a year for me to finally see if I had what it took to be a running back. I wanted to see if I could prove to myself that I was a true running back and that I could possibly play college and professional ball as a running back.

At 5 feet 10 inches, trying to be a defensive linebacker in the pro's would have been a bit unrealistic. To play linebacker professionally, I would at least have to have been 6 feet tall with about 40 to 50 more pounds added. Most professional running backs were about my height or maybe a few inches taller, so this was a position that I could actually fit in with if I ever did make it to play professional football. So, my senior year was more of a year for me to find my natural position heading forth to college and hopefully playing professional football one day.

Giving what I could to pursue my football career I tried out for a local semiprofessional football team. Trying out for my first semi pro football team I made the cut and landed the starting running back position. After our third game of the season, our team could not afford the funding and unfortunately, we had to cease all football operations. It was bittersweet for me because this was only going to be my second year to ever play the running back position and I was starting to get good at it.

Becoming good friends with our head coach I landed a position working for his concrete business making some pretty good money at the time. My coach was also the same guy who pointed me in the direction of the new semi-pro team I'd be playing for once our team ceased all football operations. I now had the opportunity to finish playing semiprofessional football, but now I would be playing in the city of Monroe, Michigan; a small town about 20 minutes north of my hometown. The journey would continue, but a new chapter would await.

Going to play ball in Monroe, Michigan I did not know what to expect. With the dream to play professional football still alive, this was my opportunity and second chance at giving it all I had in football hoping to be discovered by the pro's one day soon. Playing semiprofessional football my first season in Michigan, I weighed a bit more than I would've preferred coming in. I had speed for sure, and I was quick but I wasn't as fast as I wanted to be. I was agile and elusive, but I knew that I could chisel down a bit to get in better shape to come back ten times better than I did when I first came in.

My first official year playing in Monroe I earned the starting running back position and really made a name for myself in Michigan. We did not make it to any championships that year, but I learned a lot by observing myself that season. My first full year of playing semiprofessional football was more of a practice run for me to see where I was at running the ball. It was my first year playing running back since high school. Finishing the season, I noticed a lot of areas I could improve on. So, I studied a lot of our game films to see what the results would have been had I just been a bit faster, or even made a person miss on a certain play. I was always looking for room to improvement.

I wanted to help our team come back better so I started with the man in the mirror. I trained very hard that off season going into my second year of semi pro football. I worked on speed drills, and agility drills. I worked on my strength and explosiveness. I looked up training videos on the internet to learn drills and things I did not know concerning football and athletic training.

My hunger to come back ten times faster; ten times better and stronger was kind of that same hunger and drive we had as kids, when we guaranteed that we would not lose a single game the following year. I had something to prove to myself, and just like guaranteeing to win every game the way we did, it was the same way I had to guarantee to myself that I would be better. That I would be faster, and that I could really excel as a running back in the game of football. I had to prove to myself that I still had a shot at the pros.

My second year playing semi pro we only lost 2 games. Both losses would be to the same team, but the second time would be under different circumstances, and in a different setting also. It would take place in the championship game. Another game for me that would take a turn for the worst. I remember it like it was yesterday. I was having a good game, and my confidence was beginning to pick up. It was as if I were heating up in a sense. I started the game off with a long touchdown run followed by a few good runs after that throughout the first half of the game. Heading into halftime my thought coming out was to put the game away and out of reach.

With everything on the line, it was time for us to show everyone why we were here. Coming out of half time and with my adrenaline still at a high level, it was now time to finish the game; or at least that's what I thought. I broke off a nice run getting us closer to the endzone. Midway through the play I took a big hit to my ribs. A hit that stole a lot of wind from me leaving me on the ground gasping for air.

Laying on the field, clenching my side, doing my best to snap out of it to find any breath of air that I could; I couldn't believe what was going on. I could not believe the level of pain I felt as I laid there on the ground surrounded by a band of teammates and players from the opposite team. The pain was excruciating and was almost impossible to bear. I soon came to my feet, able to walk myself off the field and over to our sideline, only to find out that I was done for the day and that my ribs were fractured. I tried to go back out to give it a shot, but I could barely run. That was it for me, I was done for the day.

We ended up losing that day. I went on to receive the league MVP award and also the league offensive MVP award that year. I even broke our team's single season rushing record that same year also. The goal was to win the championship game but that didn't happen. It was a devastating feeling for us all. All the hard work we put in only to come up short. It was back to the drawing board to try again next year; but with fractured ribs my body would need to heal first before I got back out on the field.

With hopes of still making it to the pro's, and now with a little wear and tear, I knew the big league would not typically pay for athletes who had injuries on their resume, but that did not stop my hunger and desire to still finish what I set out to do. The fact of the matter is, suffering that rib injury, I didn't come back the same player as I were the year before. I was not terrible, but my ribs were not yet fully healed therefore my body was limited to what it could do. We would make it as far as the conference championship game before we lost and were done for the year, but I did in fact still receive the "running back of the year award," that following year also.

Over the next few years of playing semiprofessional football, I went to a couple of professional tryouts. I tried out for a professional team in the Canadian league, and also for an arena football team in Cleveland Ohio, to which I got no response from either. With the hope of making it to play professional football now dwindling down, I later tore my MCL to make matters worse! If there was any fighting chance left of me playing professional football, then that MCL injury had just about sealed the deal for me. It was time to hang up the dreams of playing professional football. A bit hurt and let down at the thought, it was time for me to figure life out. Life beyond football; and it was around that time when it all began to click!

CHAPTER 5

WHEN IT CLICKED!

"The Capacity to Learn"

Over time I held quite the number of jobs. All of which, in one way or another has made an impact on me in life and in business. I caddied at a private country club for roughly 11 years. I've sold high end vacuum cleaners. I worked in retail, I worked at fast food restaurants, and I even held a janitorial position at a church I used to attend. I worked in a popular auto part retail store. I was an assistant manager at a gas station and a department manager at one of the biggest retail stores in America; I'm sure most of you shop there today!

For me, jobs were not hard to land. There are jobs everywhere. An entrepreneur at heart, and only knowing football, I did not know that each of these jobs were cultivating me for a bigger purpose. They were creating potential in me that was adding to my value as a person. I did not know that there would be things for me to learn at each job that I would apply to my everyday life, and in business years later. To be honest, whenever there was a company that I did like, I would do my best to work my way up, promotion after promotion. Seeing a future for myself within a company, I would always try to climb the ladder, (in terms of chain of command.)

I had experience in the concrete business, from working for a coach of mine who owned his own concrete company. We worked on residential properties along with a few commercial properties. I learned a lot in that short time of laying concrete. I also worked for a landscape company and signed up for a couple "pyramid schemes," in hopes of getting rich in just a year or two. I was ambitious, and even though I was not raised on money, by this time I had seen enough people with it that I knew it was not impossible to attain.

Although none of these jobs made me a millionaire, it was the journey that I respected the most; and timing to me was everything. In one way or another being a part of so many jobs, gaining so much hands-on experiences, and being active in so many different markets have all shaped me to take the initiative to start my own business. Using what I knew, the knowledge, the experience, the training, the business strategies and techniques, the business methods, and the knacks and niches I now possess concerning business marketing and entrepreneurship; using all these things and applying each in its own way, to my own business, and in today's market.

Growing up I never knew how money worked, nor could I even begin to explain to someone how money came into existence. Money was just something I knew that could be obtained by working a job and could be spent on things someone either wanted or needed. That is pretty much all I knew about money. Everything I learned about business, money, economics, and things like that, I basically acquired from my own research or personal experience.

I was always diligent and hard working. Although I did not do everything perfect, I approached every job and every company that I was an employee for, as if the company itself were my own. I took care of the very little things, the fine details of a business; things that get overlooked sometimes. This gave me the humility to be able to know that I was not necessarily working for someone else's company; but that in a way, I was working for myself. In all actuality I was being prepared to run my own business one day. Working as a caddy for 10 plus years I observed and took notes from successful people from all over. Anything they were willing to share, I was willing to learn. Being a caddy at such a young age is what launched my desire to understand money and wealth. Although it would take me asserting myself to acquire this knowledge and experience firsthand, none the less I acquired it.

A product of the environment, by the time I was seventeen years old, I graduated high school. I went from elementary football to caddying, and now at seventeen years old I was in college for the first time. A long way from home, in Buffalo, New York trying to figure life out, the journey began. An entrepreneur at heart, a diamond in the making, against all odds I would become what I was destined to be; "a Pyoneer." Learning about passive income and residual income, and why 95 percent of all businesses fail within the first 5 years. Learning about commercial advertisement spending's, and word of mouth marketing; I was being seasoned for a bigger plan that would later reveal itself.

Learning to write a business plan, and purchasing that book my sophomore year in college about becoming a millionaire in real estate. Transferring to different schools, and taking that assessment test that determined which course of study I should major in, (business entrepreneurship, along with a minor in business marketing.) Taking that accounting class, learning about assets, and liabilities; and getting a bit of intelligence about credit and debit knowledge. Dropping out of college, and getting back to football for the love of the game, suffering an injury and finally being able to walk away from football. Then it clicked!

Everything I had been going through and learning up until this point was for me to combine it all together, start my own business, create my own clothing line, develop my own fitness app, and to compose my own book. All things I never had in mind to accomplish while growing up; more so because I was all about football. By the grace of God, thoughts and ideas began to infiltrate my mind. By the time I had everything written and planned out, aside from the business itself; I noticed that I now had a stream of residual income. Only hearing the words "passive income" and "residual income" in the conversation that day my freshman year in college; I never thought I myself would be making any kind of residual income aside from joining the business he was pitching me at the time.

I went on to map out exactly how I was going to market, advertise, promote and outsource the book, the clothing line, and the fitness app. I used all the knowledge I knew concerning outsourcing and distribution. I did my best to cover every corner as best as I could. Anything I did not know, I could do my own research to learn whatever it was, and if not, I could adapt and adjust, by learning from my mistakes and learning on-the-go.

Reading the book I purchased in college about real estate intrigued me so much that I looked up more real estate gurus, all having their own expertise, their own knacks and niches and their own business knowledge and strategies as to what the best ways to make money in real estate were. It inspired me to read and order other books also. I learned about wholesale, fixing and flipping, and even gained knowledge concerning contracts and terms. I learned about bird-dog fees, assignment of contracts, ROI's (return on investment,) appraisals and appreciation; equity, inflation, interest rates and all sorts of things concerning the real estate business.

I learned about real estate cycles, (up market, down market, peak market, and bottom market.) I learned about financing in the housing industry which gave me a better understanding of what financing meant. I learned about mortgages, foreclosures, lease purchases, sheriff sales, and much more. Real estate enlightened my understanding that it was one of the best and safest ways to invest money. That annually (year after year,) the real estate market was the only guaranteed market that was promised to increase over time. I learned that people will always need a place to sleep, and also a place to conduct business which ultimately, "commercial and residential properties" would be needed to accommodate that demand.

I learned that everywhere we walk, even the streets we drive on, are all owned by someone, and are all taxed also! I learned that no matter what cycle real estate is in, you could bet your bottom dollar that a piece of property will go up in value the following year or in years to come; keeping in mind interest rates and inflation also which are also major components in real estate to consider. Studying real estate for the years I did I also noticed that almost everything has to do with everything. That whether we see it or not, all things are working together, and that if we are still and observant enough, we can notice it all.

Or at least that's what was happening for me. Everything coming back full circle and working out for me to start my own business. I would have never thought that inflation had any effect on the real estate market the way it does. I would have never known that education, construction, and businesses in local areas, each had its own role regarding the real estate market. Even the automobile market, politics, and education were also considering factors. To have a good economic grasp on these things and being caught up with current events were things I saw that could further enhance my business intelligence, setting me apart from others. Acquiring all of this knowledge really encouraged me to think outside of the box.

My capacity to learn began to fascinate me as I dug up information on the internet and looked up more knowledge training videos. I felt as if I were taking myself to school all over again, but concerning the things "I wanted" to learn. I was learning the power of technology, and social media, using the internet as a resource for whatever I possibly could. Also utilizing any other resource I could, such as: a person, a phone, a laptop, a library, a car, a bus, or whatever resource I could that would help me accomplish whatever at hand it was that I needed to accomplish. I was learning in depth about branding, marketing, advertising, promoting, outsourcing, and learning how to exhaust all of my resources. From experience, I already acquired much business knowledge in all the other areas I needed to know in order to run my own company today. I was now more than ready and capable of acting on all the ideas and business ventures that were coming to mind.

To be honest, there's not enough pages in this book for me to discuss everything I have learned over time concerning business, marketing, and entrepreneurship. There is too much knowledge and experience acquired over time that I have, and I am afraid some of it would bore you all. Therefore, I am doing my best to keep it simple and straightforward, jumping right into the core experiences, and the core teachings that have particularly cultivated my mind to think the way it does today. Things that will allow you to profit and benefit form most, in terms of what you can and will take from this read. I am trying to keep all unnecessary information apart from this book, and only what I feel you can use, profit, or benefit from now. I am trying to give you the mind of a Pyoneer.

The Pyoneer clothing brand itself came full circle for me. Initially I did not make the brand to sell. I just wanted a clothing brand that I could relate to that would motivate and inspire myself. It was going to be a different name, but I found out that the name of that brand had already been taken. Therefore, the only thing I could think of that made any sense, was when a friend from my hometown called me the pioneer of semi pro football. He said that I was going to be the reason we all made it to play professional football. It stuck with me ever since, and years later I changed the spelling and used that word as the base name for my first clothing brand. Everything from the logo, all the way down to the meaning itself, it all came full circle, and was all destined in a way. It all had a purpose. A purpose even bigger than I knew or even know now for that matter.

Being that I worked many jobs I was able to gain work experience in different industries. I was a manager at a big retail store learning how to run two departments at once. My job involved me understanding my department's rate of sales, (daily, weekly, monthly, and annually.) I learned mark up's, mark down's, clearance sales and prices changing. I gained knowledge concerning floor plans and planograms, and how to strategically plan for holidays and current events. I was required to understand my department's inventory and merchandise, (knowing how many products and items we had on-hand in our inventory,) using a handheld electronic device that kept track and calculated all this information.

We were to know the quantity of products that were in our inventory. We were to know how many items we should have on the sales floor and how many we should have in our backroom. Every time we pulled items from the backroom storage, we would have to scan it all, thus further keeping track of all the inventory. By the time I started my business, my bank offered me this same technology and I can now use my own handheld electronic device to monitor and calculate my own inventory and sales transactions today.

Being a department manager also taught me how to order more products according to the number of product purchases we took on. Since we could track our rate of sales this meant we had an exact number as to how many sales a certain item sold a year ago from the day, the week, or the month. For example, if I knew I sold 5 units of a certain item this day last year, then I knew that I needed at least 5 units (on hand,) this same date a year later. Our hand-held system was so precise, a good manager could further increase sales, simply by having each product a customer or guest was coming to purchase available and on-hand every day. If we did not have a product on hand by the time a customer or guest came to purchase it, then we were losing money. Even further if we were out of a certain product, we could miss out on an opportunity to possibly "up sell" featured items. Meaning, perhaps the item that happened to be out of stock was possibly the featured product of a different item a guest wanted to purchase. Without the product on hand this meant that we would miss this opportunity to serve our guest; which isn't good for business.

This handheld electronic device system helped us manage and advance the company's profit. We could also plan and make our inventory orders accordingly, anticipating peak days and also peak season. As department manager's we were managing a store within a store, and we had the authority to do just that. I had the ability and authority to make new purchases from vendors that came in pitching us about new products of which we may not have had at the time. I could make this decision based on the profit margin, the quantity, and a few other factors. Ultimately, it was my decision to determine if the vendor's product was an asset or liability to my department.

Asset protection and loss prevention were a couple other key things I learned in managing a business. Knowledge on how to account for theft and damaged products, along with returned items. Shipping and handling knowledge, I gained from almost every job I worked for. Still eager to be precise in my doings, I did my own distribution research for my own company. Learning how I was going to outsource, ship and distribute the products from my company around the world.

I remember landing a position as a package handler for a shipping company, around the time I started my own business. I was still playing semi pro football. It was this time when I started having ideas left to right concerning business. I remember a lot of friends and family asking me if I could train their children in football. That is when the idea to open a training facility and a sports agency came to mind. In fact, there were a lot of other ideas and business ventures that came to my mind, but due to copyrights and legalities still being in the works, I cannot disclose all of these ventures.

I wanted a training facility because I could not control the conditions of the weather when I trained athletes outside. I figured that if I do train student athletes, that there was no purpose of me sending them off to sign a contract with some sporting agency that didn't even know their true talent or potential; thus the reason I looked into starting my own sports agency. I wrote a list of businesses and came up with a plan to bring all these businesses about. I engineered a plan, creating a business vehicle from scratch that would provide its own residual income, profit, and streams of revenue, that would ultimately fuel itself. A business vehicle that would be based on the success of the clothing line, the fitness app, the book I am now writing, along with buying and selling cars while being active in the real estate market.

These four base streams of income are what the enterprise would run on. The engine would compose of the trail of subsidiary companies I had in mind. I had hundreds of businesses and ideas in mind that would all be financed by these initial base streams of income. Holding the vehicle together would be the knowledge, the experience, and the firsthand training I acquired over time. The knacks and niches I picked up. The business strategies, techniques, and methods I now possess as a cultivated and seasoned business owner myself. This would all hold my business vehicle together. It is what I planned on using in terms of managing and scaling my entire business.

Working as a package handler I had a talk with one of our dock supervisors. If I remember correctly, I was extremely business hungry and anxious to learn whatever I could. I was assigned to his dock for the day, and I was unloading one of his trailers. For some reason I was good at reading people. I could get a sense of who they were within the first 30 seconds of meeting them. I figured he knew a bit about business, so confidently enough, I walked up to him and asked if there was anything he did outside of the supervising position he held at our job.

I was hoping he could sense the business aroma a young man like myself carried around, intrigued to acquire business knowledge outside the four walls of our workplace. Immediately he opened his phone and began to explain how he owns his own business and what exactly it is that they do specifically. I was astonished. It was all coming at me fast because although I did not have a business yet, I too was a businessman, an entrepreneur at heart, and he was definitely speaking my language.

He stated that he has a bit of business in the gold refining business. I never knew much about gold at the time. I did not know the value of gold and the backing of money thereof. I was intrigued and eager to learn more. I was adding this to my knowledge resume in hopes of doing business in the gold refining market one day soon. I learned more about gold through my own research. Things like understanding how and why our country is in so much debt. At the time, and before I did my own research about gold, all I knew about gold was that it was appealing to look at, and that it cost a lot. I could not tell you how gold was made or anything worth telling you for that matter.

My supervisor went on to show me pictures of gold nuggets that their refining company had dug up. He showed me documents containing the weight of the gold they were finding (in kilos.) He showed me the price and the business transactions he and his partners were dealing with also, and it was all blowing my mind! Silly enough, before seeing the refinery process, I thought gold really came in bars of gold. I knew it had to be melted down, but I never saw the entire process with my eyes. Seeing pictures of small and thick chunks of gold being dug up and found was an eye opener for me.

My supervisor went on to explain how I could possibly get active in the gold refining business, but it would first take a bit of money to get started. I remember thinking of a few shows I saw on television that made all this a bit clearer. One was about the gold rush and the things that took place during. The other show was about refining companies digging for gold. With all this in mind, and later doing my own research I had a better understanding of the gold business now, and I figured once I had the means, I would become active in gold investing.

I knew sports, football, real estate, how to write a business plan, and I was an entrepreneur at heart. I had a semester of accounting knowledge, and now I was being introduced to the gold industry. My supervisor encouraged me to take his number in hopes of us sitting down to talk more outside of work. Although I was business minded, I did not have any type of plan conducted at the time.

Being that he was not my direct supervisor, this made it easier for me to avoid him after our conversation that day. I say avoid, because I did not have anything to present besides a bit of real estate knowledge and the heart of an entrepreneur. I did not want to waste his time nor mine, but even then, trying to avoid him was actually harder than I thought it would be, because we would always find ourselves running into one another while at work. Every time he saw me, he would say: "You still haven't called me yet." By the third or fourth time of this happening, I had to explain to him that the reason I haven't called, is because I had no business plan, no presentation of business or anything to present in that regard. I added that everything was in my head and that I hadn't put things into plan or action yet. That's when he responded by telling me that he went to school for things like this and that he could help me write my business plan.

A relief to hear, and as much as I wanted to take him up on his offer, I am big on initiative and first impressions. I wanted to construct as much of the business plan as I could by myself, before I met with him for help to write it. College had already prepared me for this. I recalled the teaching I learned in that business 101 class my sophomore year in college. I would first need to go watch a few more videos and also look up a few business plan templates on the internet just to touch up on my knowledge before getting started. I wanted to see different business plan layouts to have a better approach as to how I would fully construct my ideas into one business plan.

I was trying to funnel all the knowledge I had, all the business experience I acquired, along with these new business ideas and ventures that I had in mind. I did not have a name for the company at the time. I remember renting a house from a guy at this time, and whenever I went in to pay the rent, I would talk a bit of real estate with him and the guys he worked with. I was almost ready to start acting on my real estate knowledge around this time also, so this was me trying to exhaust my resources the best way I knew how.

I wanted to learn as much as I could from these guys. To extract their knowledge and expertise concerning real estate and anything else that could help me grow in the real estate market and in business as well. My landlord made sure to hand me his business card before I left his office one day, and I will never forget it. As I was about to walk out the doors of his office my entrepreneur switch flipped on. I turned around and to ask him about his business card regarding the words he chose to place on it. It read his last name followed by the word "enterprise."

I asked him if he could explain to me what the word enterprise meant. I also asked would he mind explaining to me why he chose the word enterprise for his business in the first place. There was another word on his business card that also intrigued me. It was the word "consultant." I asked how and why did he use the word "consultant" also? I was writing my business plan by now, attempting to start my own business, and I was trying to figure out what I was going to name my company, how to structure it, and what expertise or market the company would be involved in.

Concerning the word "enterprise," in a brief statement, he stated how almost anything could be an enterprise. He further gave me a few examples to help me better understand this. He stated that he was a real estate investor and consultant, and added that people could consult in anything they know or are experts in. I suddenly knew how I wanted to structure my business. I knew how I could strategically implement everything I knew into one overhead, one business, and one enterprise. It was now time for me to align everything the way I knew how. It was time to write, construct, and put together the business plan and the blueprint that would bring all my ideas to life. It was time to start laying the foundation.

I wrote down almost 100 businesses and divided them all between two sides. On one side, it was "Phase 1" and on the other side it was "Phase 2." Both sides were a compilation of businesses I spend my everyday dollar with, or businesses that I may have spent money with prior to today. The list was also compiled of businesses I wanted to start in today's present market.

Working a job and trading my hours for dollars was fine and all. It was having no funds in a matter of days that did not sit well with me. So that's kind of where "phase 1, and phase 2" stemmed from. There was this feeling for me, that by the time I received my paycheck it felt as if 100 people simultaneously reached into my pockets as soon as I got paid, leaving me with nothing in a matter of days. It made no sense to me because here I had no product, no service, nor any other business at all that allowed me to reach into even one person's pocket.

Therefore, I decided that my business would be a company that would host a trail of subsidiary companies. Everywhere I used to spend my dollar, I now had plans on owning my own, in order to spend my money within my own companies. The Burrell Enterprise would operate in real estate, buying and selling cars, marketing, investing, stocks & bonds, banking, gold, business and financing, and the other business ideas that were in phase 1 and phase 2. The enterprise would also operate as consulting advisors, having business in sports and music as well. The idea was "ownership". Teaching my community business, and how to grow and thrive as an economy.

So, with all this at hand I began writing and constructing the business plan. The "state of purpose," for the Burrell Enterprise is that: "We cultivate the progression of the economy through knowledge, business and innovation, creating opportunity for growth and expansion." As I began to write the business plan, more ideas came to mind. Staying true to what I knew, (my heart and my passion,) is what led me to my journey of being cultivated and the process thereof. I was following my football dreams, the only thing I knew at the time; the only thing I wanted to do in life.

The rest seemingly worked itself out. Now with a business plan all written out, and a book to go further in depth with everything; I can now always refer to the business plan, as well as this book to see where I am. To see the results and what I've accomplished thus far. Also, to analyze what the next steps of the plan should be. I can now get active in the real estate market and begin starting the other business ideas I have in mind. Lastly, during this time, a friend of mine and I had agreed to do 500 push-ups a day together. We agreed to hold one another accountable through text messages. He would send text messages every time he did 50 push-ups, up until he reached 500 total for the day. The guy was a machine, and I could barely keep up. So much so that I just stopped texting him back, but he did not stop texting me. He continued to hold himself accountable, without my help.

That is when it hit me. Another idea came to mind; a "Push-Up Challenge" app! I went on to work out the logistics of how I wanted the app to look and function. I saw a push-up challenge app, that could even be a fitness app. Something that could possibly be an exclusive, creative, and exciting way for people to get fit, stay fit and have fun, while it all is being held together through accountability. It would be a new and exciting way for people to work out and challenge one another at getting and staying fit.

Altogether, I now not only have a business and the knowledge to sustain it and scale it into the business it could possibly be; but I now have a solid product to offer! Whether it will be flipping cars, selling real estate, selling clothes in the fashion industry, or even if it were marketing this book or monetizing the advertising revenue from the push-up challenge fitness app; I NOW HAD A SOLID PRODUCT TO OFFER! A product to brand, market, advertise, promote, outsource, and ultimately a product to sell!

I now had service to offer also, a business to run, the knowledge to do so, and a plan to accomplish it all. It was now time to implement everything I knew. To assert everything I learned over time, applying it all to building my own company. It was time to learn on the go; to adapt and adjust, learning from my mistakes along the way. It was time to act on a leap of faith and see how everything worked out.

CHAPTER 6

IMPLEMENTATION STAGE

"Asserting, Adapting & Adjusting"

Going forth with everything I had learned by now, and putting it all into action did not come easy. I was not promised by anyone that any of this would succeed or work out. There was no guarantee that any of this would prosper. I built it all on my knowledge along with the things I experienced over time. I built it on faith honestly. It was all a risk that I would have to take to find out for myself how everything would turn out. It was either that or live life never knowing what could have happened.

I could not trust my knowledge alone to get the ball rolling. I had to use my own money from my own paychecks. If I truly believed in what I knew and what I was planning, I would have to finance it all myself before I could start making any profit from anything. Being fully persuaded that everything I planned could work, I set out to give it my all.

If and doubt there were a chance I could fail at anything I was attempting to pull off, then at the very least I would swing as hard as I could in hopes of making it all happen the way I envisioned. I was not going to leave any doubts or be left with any regrets. It was like I had nothing to lose because I was already accustomed to the working life. Working a job was the normal thing to do in life, and I already had my fair share of job experiences. I knew how far they got me in life as opposed to where I wanted to be, and where I knew I could be in life.

I started writing and constructing the business plan in October 2019 and had it complete and finished sometime by the end of November 2019.

I had all my logos for every business idea all drawn up also. I remember it was in the month of December 2019, when I made up my mind to fully go after what I had been learning and preparing to do. The business structure and the direction I wanted it to go, was now formed and ready for takeoff.

Understanding technology and resources played a big role, as it came to me taking my first steps at asserting what I knew. Before I got started, I would need to get the latest and best tech phone and laptop I could possibly afford at the time. I paid attention to the signs in life that gave hints, foreshadowing the idea that economically we were transitioning into a digital and tech world. To say the least, society itself was looking to move in a direction that would all be based around the internet and technology, and ultimately an ecommerce business would be needed in these days.

I knew that if I at least owned a nice phone and a nice laptop, that I could do business anywhere across the globe. With a phone and a laptop, that would cover the internet and technology part of what I knew and what I was building. If necessary or needed, I would go to the library to handle anything that I could not accomplish from my personal phone or laptop. The money I made from jobs, aside from bills and priorities, all went towards business expenses.

I knew that most social media platforms would require their users to have an identification name along with a password. Also, that most sites when "subscribing to," would also need your cell phone number, along with an email address. I already had a phone and a laptop, so my next step was to create emails for each platform and business market that I would now be operating in. I would also need a valid "business email address," something I knew nothing about prior to any of this. I needed an email for my sports business, the clothing line, the enterprise, and a few other business ideas I had in mind. I would use these emails for all the websites and platforms I would soon have to be operating on. From then it was time to legitimize the business.

With all this being a first-time thing for me, I was not sure how to go about any of this. I had no real hands-on knowledge or any experience of running my own business. I was not quite fond of how a business even becomes a legitimate business. I did not know about LLC's, LTD's, S-Corp's, C-Corps, profit and non-profit organizations. This too was all foreign to me. The only bit of knowledge I had in this area took place several years ago, when my father needed me to look up LLC information for his lawn care business. He wanted me to help him start his own lawn care service, but that didn't get far because, at the time I never heard of an LLC, and I had no clue where to start. I never got to help him out, nor did I get the chance to gain the proper knowledge at the time.

Finding out how to legalize my own business meant I had to do my own due diligence, researching and finding out how to do it all. I reached out to people who I knew personally that had started a business of their own. I needed to learn everything I could so that my business litigations were properly taken care of. I needed to be operating as a full and complete business and nothing less. Learning what I could, I chose to get a few LLC's to start things off. I had a business, a clothing line, logos and lots brand's that all needed to be patented.

Therefore, everything I needed to do would all have to have been done strategically and precise; especially considering the amount of capital I had to work with. I got an LLC for the enterprise, the clothing line, and the sports business. I was starting to take boxing a bit more seriously, so I got an LLC for my boxing nickname as well. I applied for the trademark of my Pyoneer clothing line since I figured it would most likely be the first business of mine to bring in any proceeds. I also filed for a couple other ideas of mine because I was trying my best to not reveal much, and I did not want anyone to steal any idea I had come up with.

Having an LLC, I also learned the importance of having an EIN (Employee Identification Number,) that comes with your LLC once you fill out the required documents. I learned that my business employee identification number was necessary for a few things; things such as starting a business bank account, and setting up my business email which was necessary for my stride account that I needed in order to receive credit and debit payments on my clothing line website. I needed my employee identification number for a lot of things pertaining business and for me to conduct business accordingly.

Understanding that our society was transitioning into a digital and tech world, I knew I had to build an e-commerce business if I planned on operating efficiently in this digital and tech world, we would now be living in for the years to come. Building an e-commerce business, I would need to be operating on all the major social media platforms that were available.

Having a business social media "business page," itself required things like an LLC and EIN information. Integrating became a key word for me at the time. A word I picked up along the way of setting all this up. I was already strategically putting together a company with only the knowledge I knew beforehand from past experiences, and putting it all together in business plan format. I had to funnel and structure the business the exact way I saw fit, all while strategically figuring out which business would first bring in any income, and also which business bank account I would need first.

Picking up on this "integrating" word I saw that I was basically doing this the entire time; funneling everything through my own business ventures and platforms. I used free social media platforms and websites to begin my e-commerce business "integration plan." I connected the clothing line website to every social media account I had, to every social media page or business account I had, and to every other business platform I created. I used each email for each page and account accordingly. If there was no way I could connect them, I would tag links, URLS, and the website to the bio of each page and account.

I did this so that no matter which page, platform, link, website, or account a person would click on or go to; that I would be able to immediately direct the audience to another platform of mine where they can be able to see all my places of business, and all the products and services I had to offer. I needed each platform in order to reach the targeted audience I was looking to reach in order to further market and outsource the business efficiently.

I downloaded all sorts of apps to my phone. Apps I thought I needed to conduct business the way I planned. I downloaded apps that were free, and a couple that cost money. I needed these apps to market and build my businesses accordingly. I had social media apps, business analysis apps, and fashion apps also, to buy and sell clothes and shoes. Apps that linked my phone and laptop together, which was another form of integration. I knew that money transactions could be completed in multiple ways, so I figured I would need to be able to receive every form of payment possible.

Every way currency was accepted these days, I needed to be active in each. I downloaded every money transaction app that I felt necessary in order to receive purchase payments every way possible. I remember being at our local mall one day, and I ran into a guy who was very intelligent. He knew a lot of things that I probably did not know at the time. It was he who first explained to me how to start a website. He was the first person to teach me about domain names, domain hosts, URLS, and things of that nature.

He touched on things like, "print on demand," and "drop-shipping," and explained how I could better operate in the ecommerce business. Prior to this, I knew nothing about purchasing website domains or starting my own website for that matter. He explained what he could and the rest of the knowledge was acquired as I went. Knowledge I gained from asserting, adapting and adjusting, along with doing my own research and exhausting all my resources to my best ability.

That same guy would soon tell me about an app that would really take my business to the next level. He told me about an app I could download that would connect me with people and businesses that offered almost any service of business one could think of. That whatever service I needed done for my business, I could now possibly find it on this app. Service's I would have normally had to pay a ridiculous amount of money for had I found them outside of this app. He recommended that I download the app to look at it, being that I mentioned to him that I was looking for a website designer and a graphic designer for the logos and brand I had come up with before going through with all of this.

I had a vivid idea of how I wanted to market the clothing line. From what I knew by then, my toughest tasks would be finding suppliers and manufactures to partner with, along with outsourcing and distribution. My initial thought was to open a store in my local area, selling my clothes and merchandise in the store, along with selling exclusive shoes also. First, I would have to brand my clothing line, and then market it before I could scale to having my own clothing store. Now having learned about e-commerce, print on demand and drop shipping, I had just the plan to do so.

Mapping out the push-up challenge fitness app was simple, but there were a few bumps along the road as I was trying to get it developed correctly. I needed more money to get it the way I wanted it to look. I had to do all the research in order to understand how to make the app available on all cell phone devices. I had to look up all the ways to monetize the advertising revenue; (basically how to make money from the app in general.)

My thought was that I could not charge people to download something they knew nothing of. Therefore, in that regard I made the app free in hopes of adding some sort of "go pro" or "upgrade" feature. I then learned about banner strips, advertisement clicks, and advertisement purchases. These were features I could add to my app that allowed me to better monetize the advertising revenue once I had enough people to download the app. Marketing the app itself would all fall within the entire plan.

Composing and outlining the book was also quite the challenge. This book started off as me questioning myself, as to how and why all of a sudden, I had become so business minded and so business inclined. I thought it would be some sort of biography at first, but after being repeatedly asked what the book was about, I really honed in to reconsidered the purpose of this book. For me, my purpose was to simply extract my business way of thinking and the cultivation process I went through that has led me to think this way regarding business, marketing and entrepreneurship; and putting it all in book form. Giving all readers an opportunity to see and learn from what has shaped me and cultivated me into the entrepreneur I am today.

Hoping that you as an audience can take whatever you learn from this book to use it and apply it in business or life for your own personal gain. Writing and composing this book I did not want to rush it. I wanted to make sure I covered every key topic that has had a part in anything I am working on today. I wanted to make sure I align and construct this book kind of the way I did with the business. The book would have to have be thoroughly planned, properly illustrated, straight-forth and precise, sticking with the topic and purpose of the book at hand; in order to give the audience exactly what I thought they could use and benefit from, without straying too far away from the topic.

Marketing and outsourcing the book would be the easy part, because I already knew exactly how I wanted to accomplish this. Writing the book, composing it, cutting out what was not needed, making the final tweaks in the book, getting it revised, edited, and published was all going to be the challenging part. I knew I wanted the book to be a part of the final stage in Phase 1 so there was no point to rush it.

I knew that by the time I finished this book the Pyoneer Push-Up Challenge app would be finished. I knew the online clothing website and all the online social media platforms would be set up correctly, fully integrated through one another, ready to move forward. I made a clothing line commercial promotional video with the intent to give my audience a better understanding of what "Pyoneer" meant and how it all came about.

With the clothing line commercial promotional video, I had a strategy to implement the website and all the social media platforms information within the video itself. This would direct the audience to all of my platforms by the time the book was finished and released. Everything would be in place and in order, ready to finally go public by releasing and publishing everything I had been working on up until then. Now all I had to do was finish wrapping up phase 1.

CHAPTER 7

FINISHING PHASE 1

"The Conclusion"

As I finish and construct this last chapter I sit here in amazement. I sit here thankful for all of you who, page by page, dared to journey with me through a series of cultivated business knowledge and firsthand experiences. I find it intriguingly ironic but extremely amazing that this is the last chapter, and even as I sit here to write it out, not only am I writing this book out; but I am also living it out. Everything I have been working on concerning the business plan and everything I started, it all boils down to finishing phase 1 as planned.

For me, everything started coming full circle around the time I started writing my business plan. Once I caught on and started to notice this, that's when things started to click and add up for me. Even as I finish phase 1, things are still coming full circle. My first job ever was me being a caddie at a golf club. I started working there in 2004 as a sophomore in high school. I was not raised up on money and was not very intelligent in the business corporate world; all I knew and wanted was football.

That caddying job I held was my first time being around so many wealthy people. It was the first time I desired more in life. I was no longer comfortable at the level of living I was accustomed to all my life. At the time, as a caddie in high school we made so much money that we did not know what to do with it aside from blowing it, spending it all on nothing. We spent it on any and everything that did not matter; things that had no value. Worst of all in my opinion, we didn't spend it on anything that brought any money back to us!

There was no sense of investing for us. No knowledge on what it meant to invest, and no knowledge concerning where to invest it. No understanding of what money is, how it works, or how it even came into existence. Hindsight looking back, this was a very sad and terrible thing. I say this because looking back from where I am in life today, seeing the things I am working on, and building my company with the budget I have; I could sure use some of that money we were making and spending so recklessly at the time.

Oddly enough, the universe would once again allow things to come full circle for me. Our caddying program back then when I caddied was in fact, a youth-based program. This meant that in due time we would soon outgrow it and would not be allowed to caddie at that golf course anymore. Which indeed we did; we outgrew the caddie program, and were now all walking into different chapters in our lives.

Several years later, sure enough, by the time of me starting a business of my own for the first time; myself and a few other veteran caddies were invited back to the golf course to resume caddying if we chose to. I could not believe it! The place that started it all for me, was now allowing me to come back to work. It was unreal! I could now return to the atmosphere that started my business desire to become an entrepreneur in the first place.

Going back to caddie at the golf club was a vital business decision for me on so many levels. On one hand, before when I was caddying, I did not have a business. I did not have the business knowledge I now have today. I didn't know how money worked and I did not know what to do with the money I was making from caddying. I was not very keen on investing at the time, aside from the time and energy I was investing to make the money; but no sense of where to invest it.

Now on the other hand, several years later and being allowed to caddie again; I have a fitness app, a clothing line, I'm soon to be a first-time author, and I have tons of business ventures and subsidiary companies to follow in due time; things would surely be different this time around. I have acquired the knowledge and first-hand experience that will ultimately allow me to grow and scale my business. I now have products and services to offer and residual streams of income also. More than anything, I now know what to do with any money I make these days and there was no better time for me to be back caddying than now.

Still finishing phase 1 according to plan, but now being able to caddy again, meant that I could network with golfers and talk business with all sorts of business people from all over. Still, there were things I needed to do within the company, (the clothing line, the fitness app and the book also,) before I could fully go public with everything. For the most part I had everything set up the way I wanted and needed it, now it would all be about the finish.

I would like to take a moment to touch on a few challenges I faced along the way through this entire experience. I do not want to convey a message to the masses that everything all went according to plan for me and that I did not face any challenges along the way. No, that is not what I want to do. I do not want you all to think this all came easy, nor do I want you to think everything went perfect as planned. I do not want you all to think that there were no roadblocks, or any adversity along the way. That would certainly be the furthest thing from the truth! There were plenty of times I felt like giving up and throwing in a towel. There were times I did not care to go on or finish what I started indeed.

Opposition and adversity were both working together and were doing a decent job in trying to bring this all about. When I set out to accomplish this all, I wanted a clothing line, something that I could relate to; something I could see in the mirror and speak to myself every time I read it or saw it. That is how the "Pyoneer" brand came about. In a way, I embodied the brand. Whenever opposition and adversity came my way, I guess it's safe to say that it was a good thing I had become a true Pyoneer by then because even though I wanted to; quitting was not an option.

Pyoneer is an attitude, or a reckoning thought with things like: hard work, grit, purpose, destiny, struggles, opposition, endurance, perseverance, people counting on you, the first among many and of course quitting not being an option. As a Pyoneer, in my head there were people counting on me to succeed. Maybe even people I have yet to meet. People I did not know that may need me to succeed. I felt as if everything I had been building was destined and had a purpose to it. With hard work and a bit of grit, I would have to go through the necessary struggles, I had to endure through opposition, and I had to persevere through everything that tried coming against me.

I knew that I could very well be the first among many. A Pyoneer possibly paving the way for future Pyoneer's. Future business owners. Future business minded people waiting to know what I know possibly. Future entrepreneurs, app developers, web designers, authors, and fashions designers. Future innovators and creators, leaders and even rulers! Therefore, when the opportunity kept presenting itself for me to quit and give up, all I could think of, was my family, my friends, and you; the people who needed me to finish. The people I didn't even know that needed me to finish. At worst, I had to at least see how things would turn out. I couldn't fathom living with the regret of never trying and never knowing what could have been.

I knew that if I failed, I would not be the only one affected by my failure. On the other hand, I knew that if I succeed, then a lot of people could succeed also, because my business was created to help and teach others. To "cultivate the progression of the community through knowledge, business, and innovation, creating opportunity for growth and expansion." When I first started writing the business plan, I was excited! I felt as if I discovered something and was on to something that was much bigger than myself.

Full of excitement I remember wanting to call my old supervisor who inspired me to construct my business plan in the first place. From a conversation we held before, I knew he had connections to investors. I thought, or rather I was under the impression that he encouraged me to put a business plan together so that he could connect me with investors concerning my business. Only to find out that by the time I finished it and mailed it over for him to look at, that none of this would be happening.

He went on to ask me about my budget and even further, he went mentioned that "things don't always go as we plan." This was not the encouragement I was hoping for at the time. Especially hearing all this from the guy who inspired me to start my business plan. Hearing this from the person, I thought, was my best chance at me receiving any business loan, this was a complete let down for me.

I'm sure he was not trying to hurt me or discourage me; in fact, he was giving me sound advice and sound criticism that had a lot of truth to it;

(hence all the adversity I would later run into.) A budget at the time did not register correctly for me when he asked me about my budget. Although I had a well-constructed business plan; I did not really understand what he meant when he asked what my budget was.

It was later when my brother gave me some money that I spent, (but I did not account for it,) that is when I got a better understanding on what that budget question meant. My brother gave me this money long after the budget question. I did not have a list of things that needed to be done, nor did I write down the cost of everything that needed to be done. I didn't even write the cost of the entire overhead of the company before building it. I really didn't even know what I was building; I was more so just applying what I knew and what I wanted to do. The rest was adapting and adjusting as well as learning on the go.

Once I spent the money my brother gave me, by the time it was gone, I could not account for it. I didn't remember what all got paid with it to evaluate the success of the investment thereof. Once the money was gone it gave me a better chance to see an estimate of how much capital I now needed to finish phase 1. I now knew how much the overhead cost for my projects were and how I could budget my spending accordingly and in a timely fashion.

I was a bit angry at myself for not keeping an account at the time, but I appreciated the lesson learned. I vowed to always have an accounting journal to account for everything in the financial department of the entire business. From then, I made sure that I wrote down all the expenses ahead of time to evaluate and assess it all on my approach, rather than just coming in hot swinging with no target, hoping to get things done.

By the time I had all the expenses written down I saw how much money I now needed for my entire project of phase 1. I knew how much I could make from my paycheck, and this helped me plan for deadlines better. Being able to see what all needed to be done, and how much it cost in order to finish phase 1, the budget question made all the more sense to me now.

All in all, I could have let my discouragement rule over me when I did not hear the words I wanted to hear from my supervisor that day. I could have given up and threw in a towel then. I mean I was speechless when he asked me about my budget. Probably because I had no answer for him. I was a little discouraged when he said: "things don't always go as we plan," and later I found out that they sure don't. He was only trying to help me that day, but I had other things in mind at the time, which left me feeling a bit distraught. My main thought was, "ok, I'll figure it out, and get back with him once I handle everything I planned."

To say the least, disappointments will occur. If you don't know that by now, let me be the first to say they will. You will have to deal with them, and sometimes even learn how to adapt and adjust to things when they are not going the way you plan or intend for that matter. I faced so many things from start to finish that could have made me throw in a towel.

My business alone was difficult to construct and put together. I didn't even know what business I would be planning for. I only knew what I knew from being cultivated. I was not sure how to turn what I knew into a business. I had ideas to start over 50 companies, but was not sure how to condense it all into one company and one business plan. I was trying to write a single business plan for companies within a company; brands within a brand. It was all a big puzzle.

Then the clothing line came, followed by the book and the push-up challenge idea. I had to do the same for these also. I had to map them all out, and plan how I would market them all. I had to figure out how to advertise, promote, outsource, distribute, scale, and even how to manage it all; this all had its own level of challenges. On top of this, I was still finishing the business plan. Setting up the social media accounts and pages. Integrating each account and platform through one another. Spending countless hours of research, and studying night after night learning everything I needed to learn. Setting up meetings with people and the phone call conversations of me reaching out to people, exhausting my resources, trying to extract knowledge from each person. Learning how to create streams of revenue through each business I set up. It was like putting a car together from scratch.

Initially the business plan was supposed to start with me buying and selling cars and real estate. With a book, an app, and now a clothing line, I ultimately had to adapt and adjust to figure out which business would first bring in any revenue. None of this came easy for a guy who was foreign to a lot of this. A guy who was not brought up on money and did not have much business knowledge or training; but having to stand my ground, I withstood and resisted adversity, and continued to press towards the goal. Everything I was attempting to do came at a cost.

Getting the push-up challenge app developed and published was a hassle even. The first time my app designer finished the app, it was completely wrong. I was very disappointed and discouraged also. I had already given him money to make my app the way I needed, (money I did not really have at the time,) but if I was going to pull any of this off, I had to make sacrifices and take risks at times. Risks I didn't want to take at the time, but I knew I had to take. This was one of those times and boy did he come up short. To get the app the way I envisioned, it would cost me more money. I barely had enough to give him the first time, but it was a sacrifice I was willing to make and a risk I was willing to take for things to go the way I saw. He explained that there was a miscommunication as to how many features I paid for and sadly so, there was nothing we could do besides me paying for the remaining features.

My only options were to do away with the entire app or come up with the rest of the money to finish it the way I drew it up. Again, a person big on first impression, I could not see myself releasing and going public with anything if everything didn't come together the way I saw it in my vision. I could not release the commercial promotional video without the book being published, nor without the app being done exactly how I saw it. I could not have one without the other. Everything had to go the way I saw it and needed it to go. Therefore, we agreed to break the cost down in payments, which meant more time would be needed to finalize everything.

I remember the problems I faced with my website, and the agony that came with that entire process. I bought my website domain name from one host, but when I paid my web designer to do my website, he mentioned that I made a slight mistake. He explained that I should have bought my website domain name through a different host. He went on to explain how he could build it better from there.

The problem with this, was that I now had to transfer the domain name from the initial host, to the one he now recommended. This was an exhausting process but no matter what, my motto was to make things happen regardless of the obstacle. Thinking my web designer could make my website exactly the way I saw and needed it to be, I must have been living in some dream world. I truly thought he would nail it for me, but just like my app not coming out the way I intended, my website came out a lot worse.

He missed on all cylinders. Disappointment would again settle in, but what can you do, besides roll with the punches and figure things out. Therefore, I figured it out myself. I designed my own website. This too would be my first time getting involved with any web design practice. This obstacle worked out in my favor, because even though my web designer did not deliver on the website as needed, it gave me the chance to fiddle with designing it myself. The way he started it and had it laid out, pretty much gave me an idea of what I could do from there, and with a little browsing and doing my own research, I began to catch on to this web designing thing.

I started building the website exactly how I saw it in my head. The knowledge and experience I gained from this were unfathomable! Creating my website on my own, was in fact the best move for this project. It led me down more paths of learning and more paths of research. It led me to learn about SEO's (search engine optimization,) and tags, descriptions, key words, and all sorts of things in this nature. All of which better helped me market my business. Search engine optimization helped broaden the search of accessing my brand, my business, my products and services through the entire internet. This also helped me understand a bit more about coding and algorithms.

I faced challenges literally from start to finish. Creating and drawing my logos were not hard to draw and color on a simple piece of paper. Getting the graphic designers to design the logo print files exactly the way I drew them up and imagined them to be was all a nightmare! I didn't think this would be a challenge. I thought as simple as it was for me to draw it on paper, that it would be just as easy for them to design the print files on a computer. Fact of the matter is, we all worked together, and overtime we got them all done correctly as needed.

Then there was figuring out the trademark and business registration process, and everything I needed to do for patents and copyright legalities. Even before I revealed any ideas or anything about the business, I was skeptical concerning theft purposes, and the security of my ideas thereof. I knew about a poor man's copy as a form of ownership and copyright for any idea a person had come up with, but was child's play.

I also heard from another friend, how much he spent on his attorney and for his trademark he had for his business. I was filing for 3 trademarks, and I really didn't have that kind of money within the budget, so I had to be wise; I had to strategize and plan for what I could afford. My thought was to get an LLC for my ideas first. Making each a limited liability company through the secretary of state in Ohio. I could then build and scale up from there until I could afford any trademark, copyrights, or patent registrations.

By the time I did have the money for my attorney and my registration fees, another challenge would await. I found an affordable attorney that was going to handle filing all my trademark paperwork, which was a relief compared to the price my friend said he paid for one trademark. I got everything paid for and taken care of and would have to wait a few months to find out about if they were approved.

Getting the results back I found out that my trademarks were all approved! I hoped and assumed they would, but I was still amazed to see that they actually did get approved. It was my first step at going beyond just having an LLC. I was becoming a registered business. I thought this was the last step in the process only to find out that I would have to pay another fee to accept their approval. Being that I was filing for 3 trademark registrations, this meant I had to pay for 3 approvals. More money I did not have at the time. Sadly discouraged, I wanted to give up yet again. Another roadblock in the way. Another obstacle within the objective. Another challenge to face.

Branding my clothing line had its ups and downs also. I got scammed a couple of times trying to make orders for the clothing line. I was working from my own expense, and putting any extra money I had back into my company. I had so many different marketing strategies and plans it was ridiculous! The problem was that I could not afford it all at once.

I had to plan each project according to my budget. I reached out to athletes from all over to see if I could sponsor them with clothing apparel and merchandise from my clothing line. To further market the brand, I reached out to models in my local area, fashion retail store owners, local businesses and more. I literally had to work all of this out, from top to bottom, and learn the ins and outs to everything concerning the entire business, and everything I was trying to build. If I say this all came with no adversity, no opposition, no struggles or disappointments; then I would not be telling you the truth.

When I first set out to own my own business, I did not know what I was signing up for. I thought I had it all figured out. I thought my business plan would make everything happen the way I planned it. I did not know that there were challenges all awaiting to present themselves at the right time. I did not know the detriments and requisites it took in order to run and manage a business to its full potential. I did not know this journey would take me to the land of the unknown; untrodden ground filled with opposition, mistakes, let downs and discouragement. I only knew what I thought I knew, and I did not want to regret not acting on any of it. I have heard of a saying, that once people live a long and fulfilled life, that in terms of "regret," they regret the things they "did not," do in life, more than regretting the things they have done in life. I did not want to look back in regret, always wondering about what could have happened.

Finally, with everything in place and set up in the way I needed it, I was ready to move forward. The plan was to release my clothing line commercial video to all my social media accounts and pages. The book and push-up app were now finished and almost ready to be published and public. The commercial was created to explain the Pyoneer brand and how it all came about, along with directing the audience and viewers to the website and all the social media pages.

The website, along with the social media accounts and pages would all have links, and would all be integrated through one another, and all being associated with each business and venture within the Burrell Enterprise. The website will have links for book purchases and app downloads, as would the social media accounts and platforms along with clothing apparel and merchandise available also.

Once released and finally public the plan is to then take any earned revenue, using it to buy and sell cars, and real estate, and also to finance every business venture I have planned remaining in phase 1 along with the business ventures in phase 2. Now that I am back caddying at the golf course I once worked at before, more doors of opportunity have opened for me. I was offered an opportunity to move to Florida for a few months to do some more caddying.

This is another opportunity that will involve more adapting and more adjustments, but the possibilities of what could come from this are endless. This could very well turn out to be a good business decision for the company. I could meet and connect with fellow business people like myself, but now in a new environment; a new state rather. The sunshine state itself. I could market and promote the book, the app, the clothing line, and all my business for this matter; all down in the sunshine state. I could gather real estate information in the area also, and still caddie all at the same time.

If all goes well, and I am sure it will, I could be back to my hometown having done enough marketing and research, to have expanded the business to another state. It could be an opportunity to get all the inventory into the three fashion retail stores I have an agreement with back in my hometown and all according to plan. This could be a divine opportunity and also a way to help fund and start the rest of the business ventures I have in mind; all in strategic order as done before in phase 1. But I guess we will have to find out what happens in Phase 2...

BURRELL ENTERPRISE BUSINESS PLAN TEMPLATE/OUTLINE

State of Purpose

"We cultivate the progression of the community through knowledge, business, and innovation, Creating opportunity for growth and expansion."

Executive Summary:
- Mission
- Vision
- Keys to success
- Location
- Potential Clients, customers, and audience

Product & Services:

Product(s) Description:

Market Research & Analysis:
- Competition
- Clients
- Marketing Strategy & Plan

Sales Forecast & Financial Data
- Projected earnings

Future Endeavors
- Scaling Plans
- Investing Plans

Implementation Schedule
- What needs to be done
- Capital Needed for overhead
- Current Capital/Revenue/Assets/Liabilities
- Budgets/Budgeting

Team & Resources
- People you know
- Places you can utilize
- Things you can utilize

INVESTING

"There's 24 hours in a day, how does your investing look?"

Things to invest:
- Your Time
- Your Energy
- Your Money

Things to invest in:
- Your Mind
- Yourself
- People/Others
- A Bank
- A Business
- Your Business
- Gold, Minerals, Jewelry
- Stocks & Bonds
- Real Estate
- Technology
- Energy
- Crypto Currency
- Paintings & More!

KEY WORDS

(ABC Order)

A's
Accountant
Accounting
Advertisement
Advertising
Appraisal
Appreciation
Apps
APR (Annual Percentage Rate)
Algorithm
Assets
Asset Protection
Assignment of Contract

B's
Bank
Bank Account
Bank Statement
Bird Dog Fee
Brand
Branding
Broker
Budget
Business
Business Conduct

Business Email
Business Literate
Business Marketing
Business Plan
By Laws

C's
Capital
Capitalism
Cash Cow
Cash Flow
Cell Phone
Centralized Currency
Clearance
Coding
Congress
Condense
Contract's
Contract Terms
Competition
Competitors
Commercial Banking
Commercial Insurance
Commercial Real Estate
Commodities
Copyrights
Corporate
Corporation
Credit
Credit Score
Crypto Currency
Current Events

D's

Debit
Delegate
Deposit
Derivatives
Design Theory
Distribution
Debit
Delegate
Deposit
Derivatives
Design Theory
Distribution
Domain Host
Domain Name
Download
Down Payment

E's

Economics
E Commerce
EIN (Employee Identification Number)
Equity
Enterprise
Entrepreneur
Exchange
Exhausting Resources
Elevator Pitch

F's

Finance
Finances
Financial Advisor

Financial Instruments
Financial Literacy
Fixed Rate
Floor plan
Foreclosure
Funds
Funds of Funds
Funnel
Futures

G's
Graphic & Design

H's
Hedge Fund

I's
Incorporated
Inflation
Innovate
Insurance
Insurance Carriers
Integrate
Inventory
Invest
Investing
Investment Banking
Interest
Interest Rates
IRS (Internal Revenue Service)

J's

K's
Knacks & Niches
Knowledge

L's
Laptop/PC
Land Contract
Leisure
Liability
Library
Liquidate
Liquid Funding

M's
Manage
Management
Margin Calls
Markdowns
Markups
Market
Marketing
Marketplace
Median of Exchange
Merchandise
Methods
Monetize

N's
Non-Disclosure
Non-Profit
Non-Refundable

O's
Online Purchases
Online Subscriptions
Outsource
Overhead
Owner
Ownership

P's
Partners
Passive Income
Patents
Payment Methods
Percentage
Personal Insurance
Planogram
Platform
Plethora
Price Change
Print Files
Private Equity
Profit
Profit Margin
Property Taxes & Insurance

Q's
Q&R Codes

R's
R&D (Research & Development)
RAM (Random Access Memory)
Rate of Sales
Real Estate
Receipt
Refund
Register

Registration
Regulation
Residuals
Residual Income
Residential Properties
Returns
ROI (Return on Investment)
Royalties

S's
Sale
Scale
Sell
SEO (Search Engine Optimization)
Sheriff Sale
Shipping
Shorts
Skills (Welding, Electrician, Carpenter etc.)
Social Media
Strategy
Stream
Subprime Loan
Subsidiary Company
Subsidies
Supply and Demand

T's
Tags & Categories
Targeted Audience
Tax
Taxes
Tax Code
Tax Liens
Techniques
Technology
Thumbnail

Title Deed
Trademark
Transaction
Trends, Trending

U's
Umbrella Company
URL (Uniform Resource Locator)

V's
Vector Files
Vendor

W's
Website
Wholesale

THINGS TO UNDERSTAND

(Regarding Life & Business)

ABC Order

Amendments
Agriculture
Appropriation Bill
Automobile Industry
Bill of Rights
Biomass
Civil Rights
Congress
The Constitution
Chemical Energy
Economics
Education
Energy (all forms)
Executive Branch
Federal Trade Commission
Free Market
Free Trade
Geography
Geothermal Energy
Gold
History
Hydropower
IRS

Irrigation
Judicial Branch
Laws & Bills
Legislation
Legislative Branch
Lobbyist
Lobbying
Median of Exchange
Minerals
Natural Energy
Nuclear Energy
Politics
Retail
Real Estate/Housing Market & Industry
Solar Energy
Skills & Trades
Tax Breaks
Tax Code
Trade Bargaining System
Trade Laws
Wind Energy

WHAT I EXPECT YOU TO TAKE FROM THIS BOOK

1) For you all to learn about Business & Entrepreneurship.
2) For you all to understand the significance and importance of "Branding, Marketing, Advertising, Promoting, & Outsourcing."
3) For you all to understand the impact technology, the internet, and social media has all made in today's society, and how to utilize each correctly and efficient for your business.
4) For you all to understand resources (people, places, & things,) and the significance of "exhausting" each.
5) For you to all become financial literate, if not more than you already are.
6) For each of you to challenge yourself to learn more; to broaden your capacity to learn.
7) For each of you to challenge yourself to assert & apply yourself more in something positive you want to accomplish or may have even been waiting to accomplish for some time now.
8) For you all to be diligent in all your doings; being quiet and still enough to see and hear what the universe may be trying to communicate to you.
9) I expect to inspire more first-time business owners, more entrepreneurs, and also to hopefully inspire more first-time authors.
10) That at worst, this book could very well just be a great read for someone, and with that alone; I'll take it.

LLC website marketing selling in
reaching out public face
Going Hard

Now/Phase' part'

- record label, clothing, marketing, Graphics
- painting, picts (Graphic design help)
- real estate - Landscape
- Graphic Design team video production
- Selling Cars, marketing, graphic, Insurance
- Clothing label P marketing, press comp.
- Clothing hub map,
- SI / online magazine pages
- Book
- Hallmart Cards
- Comic Books
- M.A.P
- Shoes flipping, Hair Bundles
- Gold
- Training facility (Day care & Dorm)
- Stock / Steak
- Self Knowledge Classes
- Motivational speaking
- Mentor speaking / Live Seminars
  (Training facilities/kids)
  (Seminar / self knowledge for kids & men/adults) cultivating classes
  (consultant, advisory etc.)

- local shark tank

Later/Phase² /Phase³

Air BnB / Hotels / App / App / grammy App
website
Architect

- yard design / patio design / Home design
- concrete   → Real estate
- Landscape
  Home Auto Life Business - personal Phone
- Insurance Agency (progressive) liscence. buy a
- Tow Truck
- Snow Truck
- Car lot financing, Autozone, fix, Tires,
- Junk yard, window com, auctions
- Sports Agency - lawyers, contracts, endorse
- Finance Company (cars + Homes etc port store (airline)
- Tire Co., car fix place, car windows, junkyard
- Boost company / progressive agency
- Jewelry Company / Tatoo Shops
- Apliance Center
- furniture + Carpet stores
- A Bank / A Mall cologne women
  get item
- Dog Kenall
- Distribution Company
- Contractors
- Manufaturing Companies
  Brick, Metal, Steel, wood, concrete
- Tools, supplies, nails, drills,
- Tractors John deers, forklifts, Babcats
- Snow plow, leaf blower, lawn mower
  Home design (lawn Seasonal Care) - contractors
  edgers, trim, weed wacker etc shovels, forks

Now Phase 'part'	Later Phase 'part'
Tax Company (filing)	- Daycare
Credit fix company	- DJing
Accounting firm ⎱ consulting	- Restaurant - Invest also mcdonalds etc
Financial advisory ⎰ advisory entreprenuer	- pressing Company (Clothes)
Self Knowledge - Business - real estate	- printing Company for (books)
- Classes = Football = youth	- Appliance Centers open + invest
- Financial literacy	- Walmarts . open + invest
- selling cars - Better business	
- marketing - Investing	- Stop n Go
- etc	- A Watch brand cufflinks watches
	- Suits ½ Ties ½ shoes ½ socks etc

79

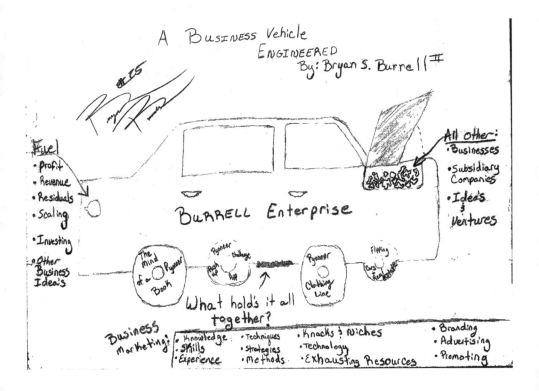

A Business Vehicle
ENGINEERED
By: Bryan S. Burrell II

#15

Fuel
• Profit
• Revenue
• Residuals
• Scaling
• Investing
• Other Business Idea's

BURRELL Enterprise

All Other:
• Businesses
• Subsidiary Companies
• Idea's & Ventures

The mind of a Pyoneer Book

Pyoneer Rags to Riches

Pyoneer Clothing Line

Flipping

What hold's it all together?

Business marketing:
• Knowledge
• Skills
• Experience

• Techniques
• Strategies
• Methods

• Knacks & Niches
• Technology
• Exhausting Resources

• Branding
• Advertising
• Promoting

ABOUT THE AUTHOR

Extraordinary, and adventurous, I was a bright and smart young kid. Talented, intelligent, brave; an entrepreneur at heart, full of courage, a leader, very influential, and inspirational to those around. Growing up, falling in love with football, I was still a jack of all trades playing also, high school basketball, baseball, and wrestling along with running track and being on the chess team for a year. Picking up on boxing along the way, and being a caddie for 10 plus years, golf also, was something I became good at. With the gift of gab, it was not hard for me to stir up a conversation with someone I met for the first time.

With a sense of humor, I could also make people laugh, which could very well be the reason I was always good in sales and customer service. It was the sports, the jobs, and the schools that connected me with all sorts of people from all walks of life. I love theatre, traveling and reading. I love training and working out at the gym. I love math, business and coming up with new marketing strategies. I love creating, innovating, and building with others. I am strong in faith, and very big on family. I speak a small portion of Spanish and I plan on speaking fluently in at least 3 different languages over the next few years.

I attended Garfield Elementary, East Toledo Junior High School, Jesup Wakeman Scott High School, Morrison R. Waite High School, Erie CommunityCollege, Urbana university, and the University of Toledo. All before dropping out, playing flag football, semi-professional football, and now starting a business of my own. Starting my own clothing line and creating my own fitness app also, along with composing and publishing a book of my own.

Printed in the United States
by Baker & Taylor Publisher Services